THE CIVILIZATION OF THE AMERICAN INDIAN SERIES

Sequoyah

GRANT FOREMAN

UNIVERSITY OF OKLAHOMA PRESS

NORMAN AND LONDON

By Grant Foreman
(published by the University of Oklahoma Press)

Advancing the Frontier, 1830–1860
Down the Texas Road
The Five Civilized Tribes
Fort Gibson: A Brief History
A History of Oklahoma
Indian Removal: The Emigration of the Five Civilized Tribes of Indians
Indians and Pioneers: The Story of the American Southwest Before 1830
Marcy and the Gold Seekers: The Journal of Captain R. B. Marcy
Muskogee: The Biography of an Oklahoma Town
(editor) *A Traveler in Indian Territory*, by Ethan Allen Hitchcock
(editor) *Adventure on Red River*, by Captain Randolph B. Marcy
(editor) *A Pathfinder in the Southwest*, by Lieutenant A. W. Whipple
Sequoyah

Library of Congress Catalog Card Number: 38–27481

ISBN: 0–8061–1056–2

Sequoyah is Volume 16 in *The Civilization of the American Indian Series*.

10   11   12   13   14   15   16   17   18   19

ILLUSTRATIONS

George Guess (Sequoyah)   *facing page* 3

The Cherokee Alphabet   40

Cherokee Phoenix   41

Sequoyah Teaching the Alphabet   56

Sequoyah's cabin in Indian Territory   57

ODE TO SEQUOYAH

(By Alex Posey, Creek Indian Poet)

The names of Watie and Boudinot—
    The valiant warrior and gifted sage—
And other Cherokees, may be forgot,
    But thy name shall descend to every age;
The mysteries enshrouding Cadmus' name
Cannot obscure thy claim to fame.

The people's language cannot perish—nay,
    When from the face of this great continent
Inevitable doom hath swept away
    The last memorial—the last fragment
Of tribes,—some scholar learned shall pore
Upon thy letters, seeking lore.
Some bard shall lift a voice in praise of thee,
    In moving numbers tell the world how men
Scoffed thee, hissed thee, charged with lunacy!
    And who could not give 'nough honor when
At length, in spite of jeers, of want and need,
Thy genius shaped a dream into a deed.

By cloud-capped summits in the boundless west,
    Or mighty river rolling to the sea,
Where'er thy footsteps led thee on that quest,
    Unknown, rest thee, illustrious Cherokee.

SEQUOYAH

George Guess (Sequoyah)

Sequoyah

SEQUOYAH is celebrated as an illiterate Indian genius who, solely from the resources of his mind, endowed a whole tribe with learning; the only man in history to conceive and perfect in its entirety an alphabet or syllabary.

He was born in the Cherokee village of Tuskegee in Tennessee, near Fort Loudon on the Tennessee River, about five miles from the sacred or capital town of Echota. Little is known of his early life, though it is well established that he grew up in the tribe unacquainted with English or civilized arts. He was a craftsman in silver work, an ingenious natural mechanic, whose inventive powers had scope for development in consequence of an affliction to one of his legs that rendered him a cripple for life. In young manhood he removed from the Overhills towns to Willstown in the present State of Alabama.

Sequoyah, whose English name was George Guess, was a soldier in the War of 1812 against the hostile Creek Indians. He served as a private in the company of Mounted and Foot Cherokees commanded by the Cherokee, Capt. John McLamore, and forming part of Col. Gideon Morgan Jr.'s Regiment of Cherokee Indians.

He volunteered at Turkeytown October 7, 1813, less than a month before his regiment under Morgan and Maj. John Lowrey participated in an attack on the town of Tallaschatche. Sequoyah's three months service ended January 6, 1814, but he reenlisted three weeks later. March 27, 1814, his regiment took part in the famous Battle of the Horseshoe that inflicted a decisive defeat on the Creeks. Fifteen days afterward, with the war practically over, Sequoyah was discharged at Hillabee.

These facts are established by the records in the United States war department and in the pension office, including the affidavit of Sequoyah's widow Sally, to whom he was married in 1815, and who, in 1855 at the age of sixty-six, invoked the record of her deceased husband's service in support of her claim for bounty land, authorized by a recent act of congress. In this proceeding, supporting affidavits were made by the Cherokees, Chief John Ross, who also fought at the Battle of the Horseshoe, John Drew, Archibald Campbell and Going Back, who knew of Sequoyah's army service and that Sally was his only widow. Throughout these records he is called George Guess.

The year after his discharge he and Sally were married according to tribal custom. The next year, 1816, Sequoyah is found at the Chickasaw council house, and there, under his English name of George Guess, on September 14, joined with fourteen other Cherokees in agreeing to a so-called treaty with Andrew Jackson and others, by which they were induced to yield to the United States a large part of their country. Sequoyah's associates on this occasion do not seem to have been important representatives of the Nation and their acts were subsequently ratified by a larger Cherokee council at Turkeytown.

Different versions of the labors that brought forth Sequoyah's Cherokee alphabet have been written, but they nearly all agree on the main facts. At an early age Guess realized that there was a magic in the written word that set apart from others those who could read and write it. Inspired by a desire to discover a

4

set of characters that could be used by his people to express
the sense and sound of the Cherokee language, about 1809 he
began his work.

Years of more or less aimless experimenting eventually led
to the definite conception of his great objective. This was a
slow and laborious undertaking, not only wanting encourage-
ment from any source, but faced by ridicule and even menace.
Finally, after twelve years of labor and discouragement he completed his syllabary. Its simplicity and adaptability to the speech
and thought of the Cherokees enabled the people to master
it in a few days, and soon a large part of the tribe employed
the new invention in uses never known to them before. Its first
appeal was to the most benighted members of the tribe, who
learned the use and value of this novel instrument before those
possessing any education or knowledge of English could be
interested in it.

The Cherokee treaty of 1817 provided for the emigration to
Arkansas of such members of the tribe as desired to remove
west and join a thousand of their countrymen who had previously located there. Among the signers of the treaty was the
chief John Jolly, who had removed to Arkansas several years
before. Jolly recruited a large party to return with him to the
west, including members of the tribe who were beginning to
take an interest in education. Among these was Sequoyah. In
February, 1818, the Cherokee agent started nineteen flatboats
down the Tennessee River loaded with Cherokee emigrants
bound for the unknown country on the Arkansas River.

Thirteen of these boats and four keel boats constituted the
flotilla under the command of John Jolly. There were 331

5

persons in his party, of whom 108 were warriors, each armed with a new rifle; they carried their household goods and other personal property, and provisions for seventy days, the estimated length of their journey based on the experiences of other emigrants.

On the eve of their departure Chief Jolly wrote to Secretary of War Calhoun: "Father you must not think that by removing we shall return to the savage life; you have learned us to be herdsmen & cultivators, and to spin and weave. Our women will raise the cotton & the Indigo & spin and weave cloth to cloath our children. By means of schools here, numbers of our young people can read and write; they can read what we call the Preacher's Book sent to us from the great spirit to all people. It is the wish of our people that you will send us a branch of the missionary schools, or some other teachers. We shall settle more compactly on our new lands than we were here; this will be of advantage to teaching our children." Many of the children in this party recently had been taken from the mission schools to accompany their parents to the west.

The sentiments expressed by Jolly indicate an atmosphere congenial to Sequoyah, interested in promoting the education of his people. On the long days lazily drifting down the waters of the Tennessee, Ohio and Mississippi rivers and toiling up the Arkansas, or around the camp fires on the river banks, it is easy to imagine Sequoyah studying, planning making strange characters on boards, bark and rocks, improving the opportunity to discuss his alphabet with his companions. The destination of this company of Cherokee emigrants was the country on the north side of the Arkansas River, near the Illinois, in the present Pope County, Arkansas. Here they settled and began their new life. And here Sequoyah also remained, where he continued his studies and contriving, and sought to interest his people in his great dream of a means for them to put their thoughts on paper as the white people did.

He had succeeded so far toward the completion of his work that before 1821 he again returned to the Cherokee Nation, taking to his people messages from their western friends in the characters thus far completed. After remaining in the east long enough to complete his work and witness its adoption by his tribesmen there, Sequoyah again, in 1822, departed for Arkansas to carry to his people in that remote country messages from their friends written in the characters which he soon taught them to read. And thus he bound together the widely separated divisions of his tribe by ties that were novel to them, demonstrated the great utility of his work, and awakened a general interest in and appreciation of it.

The American Board of Commissioners for Foreign Missions reported in September, 1825, that correspondence in Sequoyah's syllabary was being maintained between the Cherokees east and those west; and that "The Cherokees have for some time been very desirous to have a press of their own, that a newspaper may be published in their own language." Some months before, David Brown, a Cherokee, with the help of some of his countrymen, commenced the translation of the New Testament into Cherokee. "Already the four Gospels are translated and fairly copied; and if types and a press were ready, they could be immediately revised and printed and read. Extracts are now transcribed and perused by a few."

After Sequoyah's invention came into general use the Cherokee people were appreciative of the great service rendered by their tribesman and manifested their gratitude in a manner explained by Chief John Ross, written at his home: "Head of Coosa, Cherokee Nation, January 12, 1832. Mr. George Gist: My Friend: The legislative Council of the Cherokee Nation in the year 1824 voted a medal to be presented to you, as a token of respect & admiration for your ingenuity in the invention of the Cherokee alphabetical characters; and in pursuance thereof the late venerable Chiefs, Path Killer & Charles R. Hicks, instructed a delegation of this nation, composed of Messrs. George Lowrey, Senior, Elijah Hicks & myself to have one struck, which was completed in 1825. In the anticipation of your visit to this country it was reserved for the purpose of honoring you with its presentment by the chiefs in General Council; but having so long been disappointed in this pleasing hope, I have thought it my duty no longer to delay, and therefore take upon myself the pleasure of delivering it through our friend Mr. Charles H. Vann who intends visiting his relatives in the country where you dwell; . . . ."

The medal, wrote John Howard Payne in 1836, "was made at Washington & of silver to the value of Twenty Dollars. On one side was thus inscribed: 'Presented to George Gist by the General Council of the Cherokee Nation, for his ingenuity in The Invention of the Cherokee Alphabet, 1825.' Under the inscription were two pipes crossed and an abridgement of the above on the reverse of the medal encircled a head meant to represent George Gist himself."

The year the medal was struck the government officially

took notice of Sequoyah's gift to his tribe. On March 29, 1825, Thomas L. McKenney of the office of Indian affairs addressed the Cherokee, Charles Hicks:

"I thank you for the enclosure of Guess's extraordinary discovery. It is doubtless an invention of no ordinary genius and entitles its author to the respect and distinction of all men, but especially of those to whom he has given such an invulnerable instrument for the interchange of mind with mind; and who, but for this gift must have been doomed (I refer to the old Indians) to that limited intercourse that is carried on when friend meets friend face to face

"I was glad to see the Delegation had honored this man by having a medal struck for him. He should be noticed; and his life for the future made comfortable, and free from the embarassments which sometimes overtake the best of us. I have had a copy of the alphabet you sent me engraved, and expect to see it in print in a few days, accompanied by some remarks, and illustrations which I sent with it, to the printers."

The Moravians who established a mission in the Cherokee Nation in 1802 were the first in that field. For years they labored under the difficulty of translating their thoughts and teachings through a medium that could be understood by the Cherokees. Charles Hicks, an intelligent Cherokee, and the first convert from that tribe, gave the missionaries considerable information on the construction and inflection of the language. He said it could not be learned by writing it down as the pronunciation was different. He tried to show them how words and syllables were expressed partly through the nose and partly in the throat. The sounds were so peculiar, he said, that no combination of English vowels and consonants could fully express them. After much patient labor Hicks translated the Lord's Prayer into Cherokee, expressing the sound of the syllables as best he could with English vowels and consonants.

Daniel S. Butrick, a missionary at Brainerd Mission, was commissioned by the American Board to learn the language and devoted several years to that purpose, with the result that "he found nine modes, fifteen tenses and three numbers, singular, dual and plural. No prepositions or auxiliary verbs were employed, these adjuncts being in the verbs themselves. Pronouns were seldom used; instead, the nouns were repeated. With the study of years Butrick was not able to express himself so as to be understood by the Cherokees."

And then came Sequoyah who, to their infinite relief, furnished them the desired medium. A Moravian chronicler wrote: "In the year 1821 a remarkable man, mixed-blood Cherokee, named Sik-wa-yi, commonly called Sequoya, came forward with a Cherokee alphabet which he had invented and which was destined to bring the Nation forward by leaps and bounds, making the Cherokee a literary Nation. Sequoyah had never attended school and in all his life never learned to speak, read or write the English language. Of a contemplative disposition, he observed, while on a trip to a neighboring village, that whitemen had a method of conveying thoughts on paper by a series of signs or marks, and he conceived the idea of inventing characters intelligible to the red man. He took up a stone and began to scratch figures on it with a pin, remarking that he could teach the Cherokee to talk on paper like the white man. He was heartily laughed at and his attempts ridiculed, but this seemed only to make him more earnest and he worked on until he had invented 86 characters, a complete Cherokee alphabet, by a system in which characters represented sounds out of which the words could be compounded—a system in which single letters would stand for syllables.

"In 1821, he submitted this Cherokee syllabary to a public test by the leading men of the Nation. It is said that the leading men assembled, placed Sequoyah and one of his sons at some distance from each other, had them write sentences dictated to them, and, having carried them by trusty messengers, had the writing of each read by the other, and in that manner tested the correctness of his claims.

"The alphabet was soon recognized as an invaluable invention for the elevation of the tribe, and in a little over a year, thousands of hitherto illiterate Cherokees were able to read and write their own language, teaching each other in cabins or by the roadside. The whole nation became an academy for the study of the system. Letters were written back and forth between the Cherokees in the east and those who had emigrated to the lands in Arkansas.

"In 1824 a young native convert in the Moravian mission named Atsi, made a manuscript translation of a portion of St. John's Gospel, which was copied hundreds of times and distributed widely through the Nation. In September, 1825, David Brown, a Cherokee preacher, completed a translation of the New Testament in the new syllabary, and this work was handed about in manuscript."

Sequoyah's alphabet was soon established as a practical instrumentality and became very popular with the people. After

11

his removal west this great gift continued to enrich the lives of the Cherokees, but its larger use was greatly due to the young missionary Samuel A. Worcester, who arrived with his bride in the Cherokee Nation in October, 1825. Learning of Guess's alphabet, which he found in general use among the Cherokees, Worcester was quick to realize its potential value in the field of mission work and education. He brought the possibilities of printing in the Sequoyah characters to the attention of the Prudential Committee, who reported to the American Board of Commissioners for Foreign Missions:

"A form of alphabet writing invented by a Cherokee named George Guess, who does not speak English, and was never taught to read English books, is attracting great notice among the people generally. Having become acquainted with the principles of the alphabet, viz: that marks can be made of the symbols of sound, this uninstructed man conceived the notion that he could express all the syllables in the Cherokee language by separate marks, or characters. On collecting all the syllables which, after long study and trial, he could recall to his memory, he found the number to be eighty-two. In order to express these he took the letters of our alphabet for a part of them and various modifications of our letters, with some characters of his own invention for the rest. With these symbols he set about writing letters, and very soon a correspondence was actually maintained between the Cherokees in Wills Valley and their countrymen beyond the Mississippi, five hundred miles apart. This was done by individuals who could not speak English, and who had never learned any alphabet, except this syllabic one, which Guess invented, taught to others, and introduced into practice. The interest in this matter has been increasing for the last two years, till, at length, young Cherokees travel a great distance to be instructed in this easy method of writing and reading. In three days they are able to commence letter-writing and return home to their villages prepared to teach others. It is the opinion of some of the missionaries that if the Bible were translated and printed according to the plan here described, hundreds of adult Cherokees who will never learn English, would be able to read it in a single month."

Dr. Worcester repeatedly urged that steps be taken to provide facilities for printing in the Sequoyah characters, and it was largely through his efforts that the enterprise finally materialized. He was instrumental in securing the approval of leading Cherokees for the casting of type in Boston in the Cherokee characters.

Finally after many delays the American Board reported early in 1827: "The establishment of a printing press at the expense and under the direction of the Cherokees themselves has been delayed by various causes; but seems likely to take place soon. The Committee have been requested to execute this business and have cheerfully undertaken it for their Cherokee friends. Punches have been cut and types cast, after the model of Guess's alphabet at the foundry of Messrs. Baker and Greene, Boston. A fount of English type has also been procured, and a press of a very superior kind. It is hoped that printing will be commenced in Cherokee and English early in the coming year. Mr. Boudinot has been engaged by the Cherokee Council to superintend the publication of a newspaper, and of such other works, in the department of school-books, translations, &c., as the exigency of the times may call for." The equipment was finally ready for shipment in November, 1827.

The American Board paid for the press and type and other equipment of the printing office, for which the Cherokee Nation fully reimbursed it. In the meantime the Cherokees had constructed a building for a printing office at New Echota, the capitol of the Nation, in Georgia. But it was not until late in January, 1828, that the press and type, shipped by water from Boston, completed the last leg of their journey by wagon 200 miles from Augusta, Georgia.

In the meantime a prospectus was issued for their first newspaper, which was called the *Cherokee Phoenix*. Management of the newspaper was under the direct control of the Cherokees. Elias Boudinot, a young school teacher of that tribe, who had been educated at Cornwall, Connecticut, was editor-in-chief at a salary of $300 a year.

Before the press and equipment were received Dr. Worcester made a translation of the first five verses of the book of Genesis. Its publication in the *Missionary Herald* in December, 1827, made it the first printing in the characters invented by Sequoyah. Preparations completed on the twenty-first of February appeared the first issue of the *Cherokee Phoenix,* a four-page newspaper, part in English and part in the characters invented by Sequoyah. In the fourth number, the March 13 issue, began the publication of the Cherokee laws enacted as far back as 1808. Elias Boudinot was succeeded as editor August 1, 1832, by Elijah Hicks, whom Chief John Ross appointed. The most nearly complete file of this newspaper in existence is one of the prized possessions of the British Museum, in London.

In the issue of February 11, 1829, the name of the paper was changed to read "Cherokee Phoenix and Indians' Advocate." This paper appeared regularly until its seizure in 1832 by Stand Watie and the authorities of Georgia, when it was run in the interest of Cherokee emigration. From that time it appeared more or less irregularly, with sometimes four issues in a month, sometimes three, two and one. After February 9, 1833, there was an interval of nine weeks before the paper appeared, and between April 17 and July 20 of that year only two issues. There were about thirty issues of the paper during the next ten months when it ceased altogether.

Subsequent employment of their printing press was explained by John Ross, Joseph Vann and a number of other prominent Cherokees in a communication of April 22, 1836 to the secretary of war in which they sought to recover it: "The Cherokee Council, held in the spring of 1835, resolved to remove the Nation's printing press to Red Clay (in Tennessee) and to issue a paper at that place, in as much as the Cherokees were prohibited from holding their councils at New Echota within the limits of Georgia, and Mr. Richard Fields was appointed editor. It became the duty of the Principal Chief to carry this resolution into effect. The Press and materials were at New Echota, and he sent a wagon for them.

"The messenger returned with information that before he arrived at that place, the whole had been seized by the Georgia guard, under orders from" Rev. John F. Schermerhorn and the Cherokee agent with the assistance of Stand Watie. From that time the Cherokees were not only denied the use of their press, but it was "used by the agents of the United States in the publication of slanderous communications against the constituted authorities of the Cherokee Nation."

Sequoyah in his western home became identified with the interests and problems of the Arkansas Cherokees and in December, 1827, he was named one of a delegation to go to Washington. The Cherokees were harassed and alarmed by the intrusion on their land of white people who stole their horses and cattle; and the credentials to the delegates directed them to solicit from the government a compliance with certain unfulfilled promises in their treaties; particularly in the matter of the survey of their lands so the whites could be warned just at what point they became intruders. Tobacco Will, John Rogers, Black Fox and three others were named members of the delegation; but Tobacco Will declining to go was supplanted by another. In Washington the Cherokee delegation stayed at Williamson's Hotel.

The principal result of their visit to Washington was the execution of a new treaty in May, 1828, by which the Cherokees agreed to exchange their lands in Arkansas for the extensive tract in what is now Oklahoma that became the permanent home of the tribe.

Writers frequently say that this delegation was sent to Washington for the purpose of making the treaty of 1828. This is not true. In May, 1825, they had passed a law threatening with death any person proposing the sale or exchange of their lands. This exchange may have been in their minds when they set out from home December 28, 1827, but the treaty was largely the work of white people who wished to get possession of their lands and improvements. However, it proved in the end a happy solution of the difficulties of the Indians and a most advantageous exchange. Guess and three other members of the delegation, signers of the treaty, wrote their names with the characters invented by the Cherokee Cadmus.

The treaty promised Guess $500 in recognition of the benefits he had conferred on the tribe by the invention of the alphabet, and $1000 to the Cherokees with which to set up a printing press in the west for use by them in printing in the Sequoyah characters. A salt spring on Lees Creek in the Indian Territory was given Sequoyah by the treaty in the place of one he would have to abandon in Arkansas.

These promises were redeemed by the government in a niggardly fashion; after nearly six years Sequoyah had received only $150 in cash, 22 salt kettles of the value of $150, three saddles and a small quantity of merchandise, in all amounting to $389.75. The printing establishment in the west never materialized. What the Indians later achieved with a printing press was with their own money.

How the government redeemed other promises to Sequoyah is indicated by a letter written June 16, 1838, to the commissioner of Indian affairs by the Cherokee, William Shorey Coodey, then in Washington on business for the tribe. This letter contains other information about Sequoyah.

> "Washington City,
> June 16, 1838

"C. A. Harris, Esqr.
Com'sr. Ind Offs

"Sir—George Guess a very worthy Indian, and inventor of

the Cherokee alphabet, has a claim upon the U. States, and desired I should give some attention to it.

"From the inclosed certificate of Genl. Smith it will be seen that he enrolled for emigration in 1818 under the provisions of the treaty of 1817, and was promised by the U.S. agent that his improvements [abandoned by him in the East] should be valued and the money paid at the Western Agency. He had two improvements and by the 6th Art. of the treaty of 1817 the Govt. stipulated a full valuation to all *emigrants* 'whose improvements are a real value to their lands.'

"By the treaty of 1819 however, the Cherokee boundary was so established that both improvements were included in the lands reserved to the Nation; still this did not alter his determination to emigrate. I do not now recollect the exact time of his removal. In 1828 we find him in this city, one of the Delegation from the Western Cherokees, and who formed the treaty of that year. He complied with all that was required of him by the terms of enrollment—abandoned his native country, his valuable improvements, and sought the future home of his people in the wilds of the west; and he took with him the *promise* of your agent. Many years have passed away and he has yet to receive the first dollar of this compensation.

"I have no testimony with me to offer as to the amount of Guess' claim, and merely state these facts for your consideration with the hope that you will instruct some of your agents in the Cherokee country to investigate the matter and report to the Department."

Sequoyah's fame had preceded him to Washington, where he was the object of much curiosity and attention. Interest in the visiting genius was increased by the simultaneous appearance of the first issue of the *Cherokee Phoenix,* the first Indian newspaper in history, which was the direct result of Sequoyah's contribution to Cherokee culture. It was only natural that during this visit to Washington Sequoyah should have been asked to sit for a portrait by Charles Bird King, the artist celebrated for his many Indian paintings, who painted the only picture of Sequoyah now extant.

Among the scholars and investigators of that day who studied and marvelled at Sequoyah in Washington was the distinguished essayist, editor and author, Samuel Lorenzo Knapp, who interviewed the Cherokee through the medium of the interpreters Capt. John Rogers and John Maw. He made Sequoyah the subject of one of his lectures on American literature, which he delivered in Washington the following winter. Extracts from this lecture were later published in *Niles' Weekly Register,* the *Cherokee Phoenix,* and other papers, and were incorporated in an article written in 1832 by Elias Boudinot for *Annals of Education,* reprinted years later in the *Cherokee Advocate,* reading in part as follows:

"No stoick could have been more grave in his demeanor than was See-quah-yah; he pondered, according to the Indian custom, for a considerable time after each question was put, before he made his reply, and often took a whiff of his calumet while reflecting on an answer . . . . Early in life he was gay, talkative, and although he never attempted to speak in council but once, yet was often from the strength of his memory, his easy coloquial powers, and ready command of his vernacular, a story teller of the convivial party."

In some of their deliberations on the subject of the written page or "the talking leaf" as they called it, the question arose among them whether this mysterious power was the gift of the Great Spirit to the white man, or a discovery of the white man himself? Most of his companions were of the former opinion, while Sequoyah as strenuously maintained the latter. "This frequently became the subject of contemplation with him afterwards, as well as many other things which he knew, or had heard, that the white man could do; but he never sat down seriously to reflect on the subject, until a swelling on his knee confined him to his cabin, and which at length, made him a cripple for life, by shortening the diseased leg.

"Deprived of the excitements of war and the pleasures of the chase, in the long nights of his confinement, his mind was again directed to the mystery of the power of *speaking by letters,* the very name of which, of course, was not to be found in his language."

Sequoyah was led to think on the subject of writing the Cherokee language by a conversation which took place at the Cherokee town of Sauta. Some young men were remarking on the wonderful and superior talents of the white people. One of the company said that white men could put a talk on a piece of paper and send it any distance, and it would be perfectly understood by those who would receive it.

All admitted that this was indeed an art far beyond the reach of the Indian, and they were utterly at a loss to conceive in what way it was done. Sequoyah, after listening awhile in silence to the conversation, observed, "you are all fools; why the thing is very easy; I can do it myself." And taking up a flat stone which lay near him, he began making words on it with a pen. After a few minutes he told them what he had written, by making a mark for each word. This produced a laugh and the conversation on that subject ended. This was enough however, to start the inventive Sequoyah to serious speculation on the subject.

He had to contend with the prejudices of the Cherokees who tried to convince him that God had made a great distinction between the white and the red man by relating to him the following tradition: In the beginning God created the Indian, the real or genuine man, and the white man. The Indian was the elder and in his hands the Creator placed a book; in the hands of the other he placed a bow and arrow, with a command that they should both make good use of them. The Indian was very slow in receiving the book, and appeared so indifferent about it that the white man came and stole it from him when his attention was directed another way. He was then compelled to take the bow and arrow, and gain his subsistence by pursuing the chase. He had thus forfeited the book which his Creator had placed in his hands and which now of right belonged to his white brother.

The narration of this story however, was not sufficient to convince Sequoyah, and to divert him from his great purpose. After the interview at Sauta, he went home, procured materials, and in earnest began to paint the Cherokee language on paper. His labors were further described by Mr. Knapp:

"From the cries of wild beasts, from the talents of the mocking-bird, from the voices of his children and his companions, he knew that feelings and passions were conveyed by different sounds, from one intelligent being to another. The thought struck him to ascertain all the sounds in the Cherokee language. His own ear was not remarkably discriminating, and he called to his aid the more acute ears of his wife and children. He found great assistance from them. When he thought that he had distinguished all the different sounds in their language, he attempted to use his pictorial signs, images of birds and beasts, to convey these sounds to others or to mark them in his own mind. He soon dropped this method, as difficult or impossible, and tried arbitrary signs, without any regard to appearances, except such as might assist him in recollecting them, and distinguishing them from each other."

Sequoyah at first thought of no way but to make a character for each word. He pursued this plan for about a year, in which time he had put down several thousand characters. He was then convinced that the object was not to be obtained in that way. But he was not to be discouraged. He firmly believed there was some way in which the Cherokee language could be expressed on paper, and after trying several other methods, he at length hit upon the idea of dividing the words into parts or syllables. He had not proceeded far on this plan, when he found to his great satisfaction, that the same characters would apply in different words, and that the number would be comparatively few.

After putting down and learning all the syllables that he could think of, he would listen to speeches, and the conversation of strangers, and whenever a word occurred which had a part or a syllable in it, which he had not before thought of, he "would recollect it until he had made a character for it." In this way he soon discovered all the syllables in the language. After commencing upon the last plan, it is believed he completed his system in about a month. He adopted a number of English letters which he took from the spelling book then in his possession. "At first these symbols were very numerous; and when he got so far as to think his invention was nearly accomplished he had about 200 characters in his alphabet. By the aid of his daughter, who seemed to enter into the genius of his labors, he reduced them at last, to 86, the number he now uses.

"He then set to work to make these characters more comely to the eye, and succeeded. As yet he had not the knowledge of the pen as an instrument, but made his characters on a piece of bark with a knife or nail. At this time he sent to the Indian agent, or some trader in the nation, for paper and pen. His ink was easily made from some of the bark of the forest trees, whose coloring preperties he had previously known; and after seeing the construction of the pen, he soon learned to make one; but at first he made it without a slit; this inconvenience was, however, quickly removed by his sagacity."

During the time he was occupied in inventing the alphabet, he was strenuously opposed by all his friends and neighbors. He was frequently told that he was throwing away his time and labor, and that none but a delirious person or an idiot would do as he did. But this did not discourage him. He would listen to the expostulations of his friends, and then deliberately light his pipe, pull his spectacles over his eyes, and sit down to his work, without attempting to vindicate his conduct.

"After completing his system, he found much difficulty in persuading the people to learn it. Nor could he succeed until he went to the Cherokees in Arkansas and taught a few persons there, one of whom wrote a letter to some of his friends in the Cherokee Nation east of the Mississippi and sent it by Mr. Guess, who read it to the people on his return.

"This letter excited much curiosity: here was talk in the Cherokee language, which had come all the way from the Arkansas sealed up in paper, and yet it was very plain. This convinced many that Mr. Guess' mode of writing would be of some use. Several persons immediately determined to try to learn. They succeeded in a few days, and from this it spread all over the nation, and the Cherokees (who as a people had always been illiterate) were, in the course of a few months, without school, or expense of time, or money, able to read and write in their own language.

"This astonishing discovery certainly entitles Mr. Guess to the warmest gratitude of his country; and, should the Cherokee language continue to be spoken, his fame will be handed down to the latest posterity." The Knapp lecture incorporated the substance of a long article about Sequoyah that appeared in the *Cherokee Phoenix* in August, 1828, while he and his alphabet were live subjects of inquiry and discussion by his contemporaries, and the quotations in the last three paragraphs above are taken by this writer direct from that paper seen in the British Museum.

"His next difficulty," said Mr. Knapp, "was to make his invention known to his countrymen; for by this time he had become so abstracted from his tribe and their usual pursuits, that he was viewed with an eye of suspicion. His former companions passed his home without entering it, and mentioned his name as

24

one who was practicing improper spells, for notoriety or mischievous purposes; and he seems to think that he should have been hardly dealt with, if his docile and unambitious disposition had not been so generally acknowledged by his tribe. At length he summoned some of the most distinguished of his nation in order to make his communication to them, and—after giving them the best explanation of his discovery that he could, stripping it of all supernatural influence, he proceeded to demonstrate to them in good earnest that he had made a discovery. His daughter, who was now his only pupil, was ordered to go out of hearing, while he requested his friends to name a word or sentiment which he put down, and then she was called in and read it to them; then the father retired and the daughter wrote; the Indians were wonder struck; but not entirely satisfied.

"See-quah-yah then proposed that the tribe should select several youths from among the brightest young men, that he might communicate the mystery to them. This was at length agreed to, although there was some lurking suspicion of necromancy in the whole business. John Maw (his Indian name I have forgotten), a full blood, with several others, were selected for this purpose. The tribe watched the youths for several months with anxiety, and when they offered themselves for examination, the feelings of all were wrought up to the highest pitch. The youths were separated from their master and from each other, and watched with great care. The uninitiated directed what master and pupil should write to each other, and these tests were varied in such a manner as not only to destroy their infidelity but most firmly to fix their faith. The Indians on this ordered a great feast and made See-quah-yah conspicuous at it. . . . . See-quah-yah became at once school master, professor, philosopher and a chief.

". . . . He did not stop here, but carried his discoveries to numbers. He of course knew nothing of the Arabic digits, nor of the power of Roman letters in the science. The Cherokees had mental numerals up to one hundred, and had words for all the numbers up to that, but they had no signs or characters to assist them in enumerating, adding, subtracting, multiplying or dividing. He reflected upon that until he had created their elemental principle in his mind, but he was at first obliged to make words to express his meaning, and then signs to explain it. By this process he soon had a clear conception of numbers up to a million. His great difficulty was at the threshhold to fix the powers of his signs according to their places. When this was overcome, his next step was in order to put down the fraction of the decimal and give the whole number to his next place—but when I knew him, he had overcome all these difficulties and was quite a ready arithmetician in the fundamental rules.

"I can safely say," continued Mr. Knapp, "that I have seldom met a man of more shrewdness than See-quah-yah. He adhered to all the customs of his country; and when his associate chiefs on the mission, assumed our costume, he was dressed in all respects like an Indian. See-quah-yah is a man of diversified talents; he passes from metaphysical and philosophical investigation to mechanical occupations with the greatest ease. The only practical mechanics he was acquainted with, were a few bungling blacksmith, who could make a rough tomahawk, or tinker with the lock of a rifle; yet he became a white and silversmith without any instruction, and made spurs and silver spoons with neatness and skill, to the great admiration of people of the Cherokee Nation.

"Sequoyah has also a great taste for painting. He mixes his colors with skill; taking all the arts and sciences of the tribe upon the subject, he added to it many chemical experiments of his own, and some of them were very successful, and would be worth being known to our painters. For his drawings he had no model but what nature furnished, and he often copied them with astonishing faithfulness. His resemblances to the human form, it is true, are coarse, but often spirited and correct, but he gave action and sometimes grace to his representations of animals. He had never seen a camel hair pencil when he made use of the hair of wild animals for his brushes.

"The manners of the American Cadmus are the most easy, and his habits those of the most assiduous scholar, and his disposition is more lively than that of any Indian I ever saw. He understood and felt the advantages the white man had long enjoyed, of having the accumulations of every branch of knowledge from generation to generation, by means of a written language, while the red man could only commit his thoughts to uncertain tradition. He reasoned correctly when he urged this to his friends as the cause why the red man had made so few advances in knowledge in comparison with us; and to remedy this was one of his great aims and one which he has accomplished beyond that of any other man living, or perhaps, any other who ever existed in a rude state of nature."

Another man who interviewed Sequoyah in Washington and marveled at his genius was Jeremiah Evarts, who asked the

Cherokee why and how he invented the alphabet. This is the shrewd answer of the Indian:

"He had observed, that many things were found out by men, and known in the world, but that this knowledge escaped and was lost, for want of some way to preserve it. He had also observed white people write things on paper, and he had seen books; and he knew that what was written down remained and was not forgotten. He had attempted, therefore, to fix certain marks for sounds, and thought that if he could make things fast on paper, it would be like catching a wild animal and taming it. He had found great difficulty in proceeding with this alphabet, as he forgot the sounds, which he had assigned to marks, and he was much puzzled about a character of the hissing sound; but when this point was settled, he proceeded easily and rapidly. This alphabet cost him much study. He afterwards made an alphabet for the pen (that is for speedy writing), the characters of which he wrote under the corresponding characters of the other.

"Sequoyah is about fifty years old, modest in appearance, and was, at the interview mentioned dressed in the costume of his country. He speaks only the Cherokee language."

Another observer quoted in the *Advocate,* said that "when I travelled through the Cherokee nation during the months of January and February, 1828, before the press was set up, or any printing had been executed in the alphabet of Guess, I was informed in many parts of the nation that almost all the young and middle aged men could read in the alphabet, with many of the old men, and of the women, and of the children. . . . . I frequently saw as I rode from place to place, Cherokee letters painted or cut on the trees by the roadside, on fences, houses, and often on pieces of bark or board, lying about the houses.

"The alphabet of Guess has never been taught in schools. The people have learned it from one another; and that too without books, or paper, or any of the common facilities for writing or teaching. They cut the letters, or drew them with a piece of coal, or with paint. Bark, trees, fences, the walls of houses, &c., answered the purpose of slates.

"That the mass of a people, without schools or books, should by mutual assistance, without extraneous impulse or aid, acquire the art of reading, and that in a character wholly original, is, I believe, a phenomenon unexampled in modern times."

Elias Boudinot related that the first he ever heard of Sequoyah and his labors was in the winter of 1822–23 when he was traveling in company with John Ross along the road past the cabin of Sequoyah. Ross told him that in this place lived George Guess, who for a year had been so intensely absorbed in his foolish undertaking that he had neglected to do other labor, and permitted his farm to be overrun with weeds and briars.

"We rode on," said Boudinot, "and I thought no more of Sequoyah and his alphabet, until a portion of the Cherokees had actually become a reading people. The first evidence I received of the existence of the alphabet, was at a General Council held at New Echota in 1824, when I saw a number of Cherokees reading and writing in their own language, and in the new characters invented by one of their untutored citizens."

The 2500 Cherokees removed from Arkansas in 1829 up the Arkansas River to their new home and Sequoyah located on the west side of Skin Bayou. His residence was in the present Se-

29

quoyah County about twelve miles northeast of where is now Sallisaw.

Here Guess tended his little farm and looked after his few head of live stock that found pasturage on the rich bottom of Skin Bayou and adjacent upland. And at intervals when the larder ran low or inquiries from customers accumulated, he yoked up the oxen to his old cart, into which he loaded tools, camping equipment and a supply of food and started north through the woods for his salt lick near Lees Creek. Here, ten or twelve miles from home, Sally and the children, he would remain for days and weeks at a time making salt. The kettles had to be filled with water from the salt springs. Cords and cords of wood were needed to feed the furnace fires under the kettles. He cut what he could but purchased the most from others in exchange for salt. The kettles required attention and when the water was evaporated the salt remaining must be scooped out and replaced by fresh water.

But he was never too busy to stop and explain the characters of his alphabet to all who came to his salt lick on business or out of curiosity to see the much talked about Cherokee philosopher, or, seriously seeking information about the alphabet, listen to his interesting conversation. Taking a charred stick from the fire and a piece of smooth bark from his wood pile, he would sit down on a log and patiently explain to his listeners gathered round, the principles of his alphabet, simultaneously making sounds of Cherokee syllables and marks on the bark that represented them.

It was the same thing at home where he encouraged friend and stranger alike to call and listen to him talk of his great obsession, his alphabet that was to revolutionize his tribe. These activities were varied by excursions through the Cherokee settlements where he spent weeks teaching the alphabet to all who would learn; regaling grateful hosts and other listeners with absorbing tales of Indian lore—and above all, the alphabet, the marvel of the age.

And thus he lived for the next ten years a useful life with the western Cherokees, who grew in numbers with accessions from the east until there were five or six thousand of them.

Sequoyah was a frequent visitor at Dwight Mission. Every week or two he would saddle his pony and ride up the military road a few miles to Dwight to get the latest issue of the *Cherokee Phoenix* that was regularly sent him from Georgia. The miracle of reading in this paper the news of his people in the East, and happenings among the white people, in characters of his own invention never grew stale. And to see other uneducated Indians enjoying the same privilege as a result of his own industry and genius was a source of never-ending gratification to him.

The bicameral legislative body of the western Cherokees, called "The Committee and Council," in the summer of 1832 took steps to establish the school system which the Government agreed to finance with the annuity of $2,000, now belated since the treaty of 1828. The Cherokees provided for a school in each of the districts and an "extra" school for the whole nation where Sequoyah would teach his alphabet to the Cherokee people, for $400 annually.

Three years later another marvelous realization came into Sequoyah's life. In 1835 Dr. S. A. Worcester established a printing press in the western Cherokee country, which was to be employed in printing in his characters. At first set up at Union Mission, it was removed in December, 1836, to Park Hill where Mr. Worcester superintended the publication for years of a remarkable output of literature for the Indians, much of which was in the syllabary of Sequoyah. Before 1861 this press printed 13,980,000 pages of books, tracts, pamphlets, passages from the Bible, much appearing as originals or as translations into the alphabet of Sequoyah.

In the spring of 1839 came the remainder of the tribe, about 13,000, the survivors of that ghastly tragedy of Cherokee removal. Then opportunity for service in a great national emergency beckoned to Sequoyah.

The recent arrival of the Cherokees was attended with perplexing and serious problems. Constituting two-thirds of the tribe, the threatened dominance of the government by this majority was bitterly assailed by the remaining third who had previously come to the Indian Territory and who were in possession of the local government. When asked by the newcomers to meet them in council and help organize a new government under which the tribe could unite and in which all could participate, they arrogantly replied that they could submit to the old government and that no further concessions would be made them.

The differences between them were deep-seated and well nigh irreconcilable. The minority faction was composed of what became known as "Old Settlers"—those who had come from Arkansas in 1829 and others who had emigrated from time to time from their eastern home; and members of the

"Treaty Party," the adherents of the Ridges, Boudinots, Stand Waties, Starrs and others, an insignificant number of unauthorized persons who had signed in 1835 what became known as the "false treaty" of removal. Against the protest of 90 per cent of the tribe this spurious document was ratified by the senate and the emigration of the Indians demanded by the government. The great majority, unwilling to abandon their beloved native land, refused to remove and were driven from their homes by thousands of soldiers. After months of suffering and misery over what became known as the Trail of Tears, and the loss of nearly 4,000, mostly children and aged, from privation, strange diet and hardship, the remainder, something over 13,000 arrived in their new home.

They were bitter at the minority who had signed the "false treaty," whom they regarded as the authors of their wrongs and sufferings. John Ross, chief of the newcomers, the great majority of the tribe, with other leaders planned a meeting of all factions at Takatokah, or Double Springs, seven miles northwest of Tahlequah. After several weeks of futile negotiation the overtures of the majority of the tribe were rejected by the resident minority and the meeting broke up on June 20.

It was then that Sequoyah brought his name and influence to bear on the critical situation. Disavowing the action of other Old Settler leaders, he immediately joined with Rev. Jesse Bushyhead, one of the recent immigrants, in reassembling the Indians present in a meeting, where a resolution was adopted calling another meeting of the tribe to adopt a new government.

The adjourned meeting began July 1 at Illinois Camp Ground, nine miles from Takatokah, one mile from Illinois

River, and a mile and a half down the creek from Tahlequah. Two thousand Cherokees camped in the beautiful little shut-in valley with its fine springs, to participate in the proceedings and listen to the talks of their leading men. Two of them, Sequoyah who acted as one of the presidents of the conference representing the Old Settlers, or "Western Cherokees," as they then called themselves, John Ross, and other leaders, on July 2 addressed a communication to other Old Settler leaders urging them to attend the conference.

As this invitation was rejected, Sequoyah individually tried again and wrote a letter, in his syllabary, of course, to his friends of the Old Settler faction:

"We, the old settlers, are here in council with the late emigrants, and we want you to come up without delay, that we may talk matters over like friends and brothers. These people are here in great multitudes, and they are perfectly friendly towards us. They have said, over and over again that they will be glad to see you and we have full confidence that they will receive you with all friendship. There is no drinking here to disturb the peace though there are upward of two thousand people on the ground. We send you these few lines as friends and we want you to come on without delay; and we have no doubt but we can have all things amicably and satisfactorily settled."

The conference was conducted in the face of active opposition of non-attending leaders of the Western Cherokees and the Treaty Party, who were bitterly opposed to surrendering their leadership to the men representing the great majority of the tribe, and particularly to Chief John Ross, the idol of more

34

than two-thirds of the Cherokee people, whose leadership provoked their bitter jealousy and hatred.

The constructive efforts of John Ross, Sequoyah and other leaders were successful in spite of the active opposition of Gen. Matthew Arbuckle and leaders of the Old Settlers and Treaty Party. An act of union was adopted on July 12, 1839, by which the two parties were declared "one body politic, under the style and title of 'The Cherokee Nation'."

This document was written by William Shorey Coodey and after its adoption by the Cherokees it was signed by George Lowrey as "President of the Eastern Cherokees" and by George Guess, "President of the Western Cherokees." These signatures were followed by those of numerous other leading men representing the two factions.

The convention at Illinois Camp Ground continued in session for several weeks, then adjourned and met at Tahlequah, where, on September 6, the Cherokees adopted the constitution which was preserved throughout the tribal existence of that nation as a basis of government and laws.

Sequoyah had an abiding and ardent interest in the welfare of his people. And when the Cherokees of Texas were attacked by Lamar and his troops in July, 1839, with the loss of 100 men headed by their brave chiefs The Bowle and Hard Mush, Sequoyah was deeply moved by their misfortune. With their homes destroyed and their little farms ravaged, 1500 survivors fled across the Red River into the Choctaw Nation where they found a temporary refuge. Here they nursed their grievances and planned reprisals against the whites of Texas. The wise Sequoyah however, sent them a friendly letter counselling prudence, advised them not to return to Texas but to join their tribesmen in the Cherokee Nation. This the majority of them did to their great and permanent benefit.

Contemporary descriptions and accounts of Sequoyah are all too meager, but it is possible to present a few here, thus enabling the reader to see this remarkable man as some of his visitors did, and to possess some of the most authentic accounts of his work. One of the most interesting contributions was made by Capt. John Stuart of the Seventh Infantry, who saw much service in the Indian Territory. He was so greatly interested in the Indians that in the winter of 1837–38 he published a little book entitled *A Sketch of the Cherokee and Choctaw Indians*. Sequoyah's home was near the military road running from Fort Smith to Fort Gibson and it was an easy matter for passing army officers and other travelers to stop for a visit with this remarkable Indian. At the time Stuart's little book made its appearance about a year before his death at Fort Wayne, he was in command of Fort Coffee. The Author has never been able to find a copy of this book and all he knows of it is a few contemporary references to it, an advertisement of the book by the *Arkansas Gazette* that printed and offered it for sale at 37½ cents, and the following extract in the *Gazette:*

"George Guess, the inventor of the Cherokee alphabet, is a man of about sixty years of age. He is of middle stature, and of rather a slender form, and is slightly lame in one leg, from disease when young. His features are remarkably regular, and his face well formed, and rather handsome. His eyes are animated and piercing, showing indications of a brilliancy of intellect far superior to the ordinary portion of his fellow men.

His manner is agreeable, and his deportment gentlemanly. He possesses a mild disposition, and is patient, but is energetic and extremely persevering and determined in the pursuit or accomplishment of any object on which he may fix his mind. He is inquisitive, and appears to be exceedingly desirous of acquiring information on all subjects. His mind seems to soar high and wide; and if he could have had the advantages of an enlightened education, he would no doubt have brought himself to rank high among the acknowledged great men of the age in which he lives. He has been in the habit, ever since he could apply his language in that way, of keeping a journal of all the passing events which he considered worthy of record: and has, at this time (it is said), quite a volume of such matter.

"His connection in blood with the whites, is on the side of his father. His mother was a full-blood Cherokee; and he was raised entirely among the uncultivated portion of the Cherokees, and never received much, if any, advantage from an intercourse with the whites. He does not speak one word of the English language. From a very early age, he has possessed a natural talent for drawing, and very far surpasses any man in his nation in that art; but he never received any kind of instruction from any practical artist. He can draw a horse, hog, deer, &c., remarkably well; and no man in the United States can surpass him in drawing a buffalo. He can also draw rough portraits, a circumstance which, connected with his fondness for drawing, contributed very much toward inducing him to attempt the formation of a type for his language.

"Mr. Guess, when engaged in the very laudable purpose of inventing his alphabet, had to encounter many very serious obstacles, and which but few men would have surmounted. No one had the least confidence in the success of his project, and thought him to be laboring under a species of mental derangement on that subject. He was laughed at by all who knew him, and was earnestly besought by every member of his own family to abandon a project which was occupying and diverting so much of his time from the important and essential duties which he owed to his family—they being, in some measure, dependent on his daily labor for their subsistence. But no argument or solicitation could induce him to change his determination. And although he was under the necessity of working much at night, by lights made from burning pine, he persisted until he accomplished fully the object of his desire. Even after he had completed the alphabet, and the art of applying it to writing, and when he was fully able to write anything that he might wish, and when he had made records in books, and kept a running book account of his monied transactions, &c.—even then, it was with great difficulty that he could induce the members of his own family to believe that it was anything more than a wild delusion.

"At length, however, he prevailed upon one of his young daughters to learn of him his newly invented alphabet, and its arrangement, she being the only one of his family, and in fact the only person, he could prevail on to undertake the supposed useless task. She made rapid progress in learning, and soon became able to write and read with ease and fluency any thing the father would write. This began to open the eyes of the family and some of the neighbors, but did not prove to be entirely satisfactory. A meeting, therefore, was held, of the people, on the subject, and by separating the father and daughter, and requiring them to write, as dictated to, by the company, and to read, while separated, the writing of each as dictated to them by others, and that being accordingly done in every instance, led the persons present into a full conviction of the truth, as well as the utility, of the *invention*. And several of the most influential men in the nation immediately learned it, and discovering all its practical advantages, recommended it in high terms to the people. From that time it spread into general use; and the people of the nation are at this day in the full enjoyment of its great benefits.

"George Guess, in forming an alphabet for the Cherokee language, found that eighty-six distinct characters would be necessary. To make so many distinct figures differing so much in their shape, as to be easily distinguished from each other, and, at the same time, to be easily and quickly made with a pen on paper, was a matter of much difficulty. But, being one day on a public road, he found a piece of a newspaper, which had been thrown aside by a traveler, which he took up, and, on examining it, found characters on it that would be more easily made than his own, and consequently picked out for that purpose the largest of them, which happened to be the Roman letters, and adopted in lieu of so many of his own characters— and that, too, without knowing the English name or meaning of a single one of them. This is to show the cause and manner of the Roman letters being adopted."

Following the great service of Sequoyah to his people in the national crisis of 1839 the next known sketch of him is furnished by a visiting merchant. His alphabet had excited the interest and wonder of learned men throughout the land and even in foreign countries. Travelers coming to the Indian Territory made a point of visiting Sequoyah to observe a remarkable man whose fame was known over the country and abroad. John Alexander, a merchant of Philadelphia on a business trip, in January, 1840, while traveling the military road from Fort Gibson to Fort Smith, stopped along the way to visit Guess. After leaving Dwight Mission, with Martin Benge for interpreter, he reached Sequoyah's home. His diary, now in a California museum, yields the following about the famous Cherokee:

". . . I found the old gentleman's farm to consist of 10 acres cleared land and 3 small cabins clustered together; his stock is 2 mules, 3 yoke oxen, a wagon with a small stock of cattle and hoggs. He has had five wives and 20 children; his present wife has 5 children, the youngest 2 years old; 10 dead and 10 alive; his son Jos 8 years old. He is apparently above 60 years of age, rather low in stature & crippled since his youth. He is of a pleasant countenance & indicates a good deal of jenius. He conversed very freely on various topics, becoming very animated when my answers & questions pleased him.

"His alphabet was the main topic & appeared to be a pleasing one to him. He informed me that at a certain time in company with several others he was engaged in drawing the figure of a horse and the thought struck him that an alphabet might be invented so as to wright their talks by the use of characters. He sujested this to his companions who laughed at him and called him a fool; he nevertheless thought of it a great deal asking others if somebody could not be found in the nation who could make such characters; they said no; he said he thought it could

CHEROKEE ALPHABET.

CHARACTERS AS ARRANGED BY THE INVENTOR.

R D W Ꮟ G Ꭱ Ꮹ Ᏼ P Ꭷ Ꮿ U Ꭶ Ᏼ R Ꮂ Ꮆ M Ꮳ Ꮺ Ꮴ

Ꮩ W Ꮄ Ꭰ Ꭳ Ꭶ Ꮧ Ꭿ Ꮁ A Ꭻ Ꮍ Ꮞ Ꭼ Ꮐ Ꮹ Ꭴ Ꭲ Ꭲ Ꮓ

Ꮯ Ꭱ Ꭸ Ꮝ Ꮧ Ꭱ Ꮅ Ꭼ Ꮻ Ꭲ Ꮳ Ꮦ Ꭷ Ꭼ Ꭻ K Ꮺ Ꭵ Ꭱ

Ꮯ Ꭹ Ꭲ Ꭸ S Ꮓ Ꭹ Ꭲ Ꮻ Ꮴ Ꭴ Ꭳ Ꮲ Ꮳ Ꮲ Ꮂ Ꮮ Ꭼ Ꭶ Ꮚ

Ꮮ Ꮯ Ꭳ Ꭰ Ꭰ Ꮃ

CHARACTERS SYSTEMATICALLY ARRANGED WITH THE SOUNDS.

Ꭰ a	Ꭱ e	Ꭲ i	Ꭳ o	Ꭴ u	Ꭵ v
Ꮝ ga Ꭷ ka	Ꭶ ge	Ꭹ gi	Ꭺ go	Ꭻ gu	Ꭼ gv
Ꭿ ha	Ꭾ he	Ꭿ hi	Ꮀ ho	Ꮁ hu	Ꮂ hv
Ꮃ la	Ꮄ le	Ꮅ li	Ꮆ lo	Ꮇ lu	Ꮈ lv
Ꮉ ma	Ꮊ me	Ꮋ mi	Ꮌ mo	Ꮍ mu	
Ꮎ na Ꭲ hna Ꭶ nah	Ꮑ ne	Ꮒ ni	Ꮓ no	Ꮔ nu	Ꮕ nv
Ꮖ qua	Ꮗ que	Ꮘ qui	Ꮙ quo	Ꮚ quu	Ꮛ quv
Ꭲ Ꮝ Ꮢ sa	Ꮞ se	Ꮟ si	Ꮠ so	Ꮡ su	Ꮢ sv
Ꮣ da Ꮤ ta	Ꮥ de Ꮤ te	Ꭲ di Ꮧ tih	Ꮩ do	Ꮪ du	Ꮫ dv
Ꮭ dla Ꮬ tla	Ꮮ tle	Ꮯ tli	Ꮰ tlo	Ꮱ tlu	Ꮲ tlv
Ꮳ tsa	Ꮴ tse	Ꮵ tsi	Ꮶ tso	Ꮷ tsu	Ꮸ tsv
Ꮹ wa	Ꮺ we	Ꮻ wi	Ꮼ wo	Ꮽ wu	Ꮾ wv
Ꮿ ya	Ᏸ ye	Ᏹ yi	Ᏺ yo	Ᏻ yu	Ᏼ yv

SOUNDS REPRESENTED BY VOWELS.

a as *a* in *father,* or short as *a* in *rival,*
e as *a* in *hate,* or short as *e* in *met,*
i as *i* in *pique,* or short as *i* in *pit,*
o as *aw* in *law,* or short as *o* in *not,*
u as *oo* in *fool,* or short as *u* in *pull,*
v as *u* in *but* nasalized.

CONSONANT SOUNDS.

g nearly as in English, but approaching to k. d nearly as in English, but approaching to t. h, k, l, m, n, q, s, t, w, y, as in English.

Syllables beginning with g, except ᏹ, have sometimes the power of k; Ꭺ, s, Ꮯ, are sometimes sounded to, tu, tv; and syllables written with tl, except Ꮮ, sometimes vary to dl.

FROM THE COLOPHON

The Cherokee Alphabet

GWY

CHEROKEE

ᏥᎳᎩ

PHOENIX.

VOL. I.   NEW ECHOTA, WEDNESDAY JULY 9, 1828.   **NO. 20.**

EDITED BY ELIAS BOUDINOTT.
PRINTED WEEKLY BY
ISAAC H. HARRIS,
FOR THE CHEROKEE NATION.

At $2.50 if paid in advance, $3 in six months, or $3.50 if paid at the end of the year.

To subscribers who can read only the Cherokee language the price will be $2.00 in advance, or $2.50 to be paid within the year.

Every subscription will be considered as continued unless subscribers give notice to the contrary before the commencement of a new year.

Any person procuring six subscribers, and becoming responsible for the payment, shall receive a seventh gratis.

Advertisements will be inserted at seventy-five cents per square for the first insertion, and thirty-seven and a half cents for each continuance; longer ones in proportion.

☞ All letters addressed to the Editor, post paid, will receive due attention.

[Cherokee syllabary text]

Resolved by the National Committee and Council, That no person shall be allowed to erect or establish a billiard table in the Cherokee Nation, without first obtaining a license from the Treasurer of the Nation, and paying into the Treasury the sum of two hundred dollars as a tax pr. annum, and such license shall not be given for a longer period than one year at a time; and any person or persons, who shall erect or establish, a billiard table without first obtaining a license as herein required, shall, upon conviction, pay a fine of four hundred dollars, for the benefit of the Cherokee Nation.

New Echota, Nov. 16, 1826.

JNO. ROSS, Pres't N. Com.
MAJOR RIDGE, Speaker.

          his
Approved—CHARLES X KILLER.
          mark

CHARLES HICKS.
A. McCOY, Clerk of the N. Com.
E. BOUDINOTT, CR. N. Coun.

Resolved by the National Committee and Council, That the resolutions passed Oct. 13th 1825, suspending the poll tax law, and the law imposing a tax on citizen property of the Cherokee Nation, be, and the same are

[Cherokee syllabary text]

A Portion of the Cherokee Phoenix, July 9, 1828

be done; he then threw his horse aside and quit his nonsense and went to work at it & in one month he invented and learned the alphabet so that he could wright & read by the use of it.

"His little Daughter who was not more than 6 years old was much with him and learned to read from observing him without any effort to teach her; all his effort to teach others was ridiculed & he was thought to be crazy; he then came to Arkansas to the Cherokee Settlement & told them of his invention; they laughed at him and said he was a liar; he told them they would find some day that it was true; he wrote many alphabets for them & returned to the East again, and wrote many letters to his friends & when they came to him he would take up the letters and read the contents to them; they thought he was crazy. On one occasion he was engaged with some of his people endeavoring to convince them; Turtle Fields was present and he had wrote the name of Turtle Fields on his book. At the same time his little daughter above named was standing at the window observing and on seeing her father write, she immediately red out what was written & when Fields heard her read his name he was surprised & began to believe.

"In the meantime the people in Arkansas began to write to him letters announcing that they had learned the alphabet and believed in it. This at once convinced the people of the East and he was called upon from all quarters for the alphabet. He wrote them off for all who called on him without charge. They offered to pay him but he said there was many who could not afford to pay anything and therefore he would not charge any one any thing. I told him I thought he had done a more valuable service to the Cherokees than if he had given each of the Nation a Bagg of Gold. He smiled and said that Governor Houston had told him it was worth more than a double handful of gold to each of the Nation. I told him I hoped he felt happy in knowing that his people were deriving great advantage from his invention; his Countenance as well as tongue answered in the affirmative."

When John Howard Payne was in Georgia in 1835 collecting material with which he planned to write a history of the Cherokees he recorded what he had heard of Sequoyah, whom he had not met but knew of as George Gist: "Gist still resides in Arkansas .... is lame—was so, I believe, from infancy .... he was troubled with a wife whose capacity was very limited and who did not enter into his ambitions. He built him a cabin apart from his family & there would study and contrive. His habits were always silent & contemplative .... to this cabin he confined himself for a year, the whole charge of his farm and family devolving on his wife. When all his friends had remonstrated in vain, his wife went in and flung his whole apparatus of papers & books into the fire, & thus he lost his first labor .... after two more years of application completed his work. All speak highly of his drawing & of his silver work ...."

Five years later, a few months after the visit described by Alexander, Mr. Payne, then visiting in the Indian Territory, was afforded the long desired opportunity to meet Sequoyah, with whom he had an interesting visit at the home of Chief John Ross. He wrote a long account of his impressions of the man, which is to be seen in manuscript in the Library of Congress. The following are some of the passages written by Payne:

"George Guess, the inventor of the Cherokee Alphabet, came

here on a visit to me. I got a brief notice of his life, by the help of an Interpreter; and then he told me there were some ancient memories of the past which I ought, by all means, to gather. I begged him to communicate them and he said he would. The Cherokee who interpreted was a short, thin, long visaged, deep voiced personage, covered with what had once been a 'whity-brown' overcoat, with vast bone buttons, of which some remained, while the fragments of the coat draped him on every side in varied fantastic shapes innumerable. He was equally anxious with myself to hear (for the Cherokees know very little about their own annals), and Mr. Ross came and remained with us.

"We were all in the cockloft of Mr. Ross's story and a half log house, where the light and wind enter through thousands of chinks. Guess sat in one corner of the fireplace and I on the opposite side at a desk; the other two between. Guess had a turban of roses and posies upon a white ground girding his venerable grey hairs;—a long dark blue robe, bordered around the lower edge and the cuffs, with black;—a blue and white minutely checked calico tunic under it, confined with an Indian beaded belt, which sustained a large wooden handled knife, in a rough leathern sheath;—the tunic open on the breast and its collar apart, with a twisted handkerchief flung around his neck & gathered within the bosom of the tunic. He wore plain buckskin leggings; and one of a deeper chocolate hue than the other. One of his legs are [*sic*] lame and shrunken. His moccasins were unornamented buckskin. He had a long dusky white bag of sumac with him, and a long Indian pipe, and smoked incessantly, replenishing his pipe from his bag. His air was altogether what we picture to ourselves of an old Greek philosopher. He talked and gesticulated very gracefully;—his voice alternately swelling,—and then sinking to a whisper,—and his eye firing up and then its wild flashes subsiding into a gentle & most benignant smile. Before long, poor I seemed entirely forgotten by the rest of the audience. First, one quarter of an hour,—then another,—and then another went over, and no translation came."

After interminable conversation between Guess and the interpreter altogether in Cherokee, Payne was told that the old man was not interrupted for fear of breaking the thread of his recollections. The evening was thus spent without yielding to Mr. Payne any of the historical material he hoped to secure; so in the morning the visitor asked to have the conversation of the night before repeated slowly and "linkistered" or interpreted so that Mr. Payne could write it down; but he had no sooner placed himself for the task than Guess said that he had not remembered the whole tradition right "but if he could have his old friend Tobacco Will, and another man now at Red River, with him, they could make out to recall, among them, enough to do the story proper credit; but, unless he could manage thus, he would rather not expose himself to be criticized by the old people, who might say he had not reported the truth"; and thus the modesty or diffidence of Guess deprived posterity of his interesting recollections.

Within a year after Payne's visit, General Ethan Allen Hitchcock, a distinguished army officer, came to the Cherokee Nation on a tour of investigation. Here he met and observed Sequoyah, Guess, or Gist, as he called him. In his diary and in a letter to the secretary of war he wrote his impressions and information imparted to him by Chief John Ross and other Cherokees:

"Guess, Guest, Gist, who invented the Cherokee alphabet . . . . Mr. Ross told me last night that he is of mixed blood. That General Taylor of Cincinnati told him in Washington City some years ago that a Virginian, a Mr. Gist, had been sent among the Cherokees on some mission where he remained for some time and expressed his belief that the Cherokee Guess was the son of Mr. Gist. That Mr. Gist was the father of the present Mrs. [Francis Preston] Blair, wife of the editor of the [Washington Daily] Globe. Mr. Ross seemed to have no doubt of this.

"I have just been talking with Mr. Payne, a young man of mixed blood living at the mouth of the Sallisaw. Payne was educated at the Dwight Mission as he says by Asa Hitchcock, who is a cousin of mine from Brimfield, Massachusetts, now residing in Illinois. Payne speaks English and Cherokee and writes both languages. He says that Gist came to this country with the Chief Jolly in 1818 and used to live down in Illinois Bayou in Arkansas. That when he set about inventing letters he was not only ridiculed but very much abused and that very many ignorant Cherokees feared that he was engaged in a league with dark powers for the discovery of something that would become a great injury to the nation. Says that Gist had great difficulty in satisfying the Cherokees. That on one occasion being distant from the council then in session he wrote a message to one of his pupils at the Council and sent the written paper declaring first its contents and requiring the messenger after hearing it read to bear testimony to it. He did so, certifying to the correspondence between the reading of the message at the Council and Gist's account of it at the time he sent it. This he says had a great effect in relieving the fears of the people.

"Mr. Payne says that Gist's grandfather on the mother's side was part Shawnee and his father a white man, so that he had very little Cherokee blood in him. He tells me he is precisely in the same situation. It pleased him to praise Gist who he says has a very good head, 'can express a great idea in a few words,' adding that he is now and has been for a long time engaged in writing a history of the Cherokees.

It is generally known that the Cherokee has become a written language, through the invention of signs by 'the philosopher Guess.' This man . . . . has an extremely interesting, intelligent countenance, full of cheerful animation with an evident vein of good humor—may be 55 or 60 years of age—habitually wears a shawl turban and dresses rudely, as if not caring for the outward man. His walk has been impaired by a rheumatic affection which has contracted one of his limbs. He has been a kind of Silver Smith among the natives and was early fond of exercising a talent for drawing pictures of men and horses and other animals. He invented the Syllabic signs in the 'Old Country' and emigrated to this country in 1818. It is a remarkable fact that while engaged in inventing the signs for writing Cherokee he was ridiculed by some for his temerity, while many of the common people took alarm and became apprehensive that he was in league with the powers of darkness for the discovery of something that was to work great mischief to the nation; and nothing was wanting but the power, to make him renounce his discovery and desist from his labor.

"I have not introduced this detail to add truisms; but to state

46

that by means of the invention of Guess the Cherokees have been furnished with considerable reading in their native language, including translations of portions of scripture. The entire gospel of Matthew and John and several of Paul's Epistles; and they have a neat little volume of hymns in Cherokee, which they sing with remarkable skill and taste. It is known that in the Old Country (as they call their former country east of the Mississippi) they had a newspaper issued among them printed one half in English and one half in Cherokee. I am informed that a Cherokee can learn to write his language in three days or even a less time."

Sequoyah's son, who served as interpreter during the Cherokee emigration 1838–39, told one of the doctors attending the emigrants many interesting things about his father. He said the thoughts of Guess were first directed to the making of an alphabet by observing his nephew who had just returned from a distant school, spelling some words, whereupon he immediately exclaimed that he could effect the same in his vernacular tongue. He constructed a hut in a retired location where he could carry on his studies in private. Constantly engaged in making queer marks on stones and bark and scraps of paper, and from morning to night making unaccountable and unintelligible articulations as he practiced all the sound forms of the Cherokee language, it is small wonder that his superstitious fellow countrymen became suspicious of him. Believing that he was engaged in some diabolical plan to destroy the nation they succeeded in drawing him from his hermitage, when they burned up his cabin, hieroglyphics and all. But nothing daunted, he returned to his supposed black art until he had accomplished his object.

47

In the summer of 1842, a few months after Colonel Hitchcock saw him, Guess departed from the Cherokee Nation. He spent some time in the vicinity of Park Hill, making his preparations and assembling a company he had induced to travel with him, whom he pledged to secrecy concerning his mission. The companion on whom he seemed to rely principally was the Cherokee named The Worm, who afterwards related their experiences to the editor of the *Cherokee Advocate* in which they were published.

They spent some days at the home of Archibald Campbell and purchased supplies and equipment from Lewis Ross in the same neighborhood. When they got under way there were nine mounted men in the party with three pack horses: George Guess, his son Tessee Guess, The Worm, and six others. They crossed the Arkansas river a short distance below Fort Gibson, passed Edwards's settlement on Little River near the present Holdenville, and took Leavenworth's road to Red River, where they arrived fifteen days later. While Guess remained here in camp to rest, he dispatched The Worm and two of the young men in the party to the Wichita village on the south side of Red River near the mouth of Cache Creek. Their mission there was to inquire whether there were living in the vicinity any Cherokee Indians who had come from Mexico. They were informed that there were no Cherokees living among the Wichitas but that there were some on the Washita River.

After twelve days they returned and found Guess very sick. He had been unable to find suitable food and though they offered him honey and venison, of which they found an abundance, he was unable to eat of them and said he desired bread, of which there was none. The Worm then found some wild plums of which Guess ate freely and he became better.

The Worm then planned to depart again next morning, four days travel to the Wichita village to procure bread and other food that the old man could eat.

"Observing me make ready," related The Worm, "he enquired if I were going back to the village? and when informed of my determination to do so, approved the plan and requested that I should go and return in my former route; as he and the rest of the company would follow on, if he should be able to ride, and we should thus meet some sooner again. While sick, and at other times, when not traveling, he was constantly writing. On the morning of the fifth day after leaving Sequoyah, the second time, myself and company arrived at the Wichetaw village, where we bought about three bushels of corn at three dollars per bushel, packed it on our horses and immediately started back. On the evening of the third day of our return, my horse gave out, but fortunately, we met Sequoyah and party. It was then determined to encamp, and hunting up a shady place with good water, a fire was immediately made and the men began to prepare some food, which he was very impatient to obtain. He ate freely of bread, honey, and a kind of hommony. After eating he felt much refreshed, requested a pipe and some tobacco; smoked, expressed himself much better and then requested to lie down, that he might stretch his weary limbs for rest. I took a seat close by him and inquired what was his complaint. He replied, that he had been taken with a pain in his breast, which extended to different parts of his body, but that he felt so much refreshed from eating, he thought he should now soon get well, by the aid of diet. Feeling so well that evening, and wishing to continue on to the village, as some of the company were anxious to buy horses, he proposed to rest the next day at his camp, and on the following, go forward to some water course, where we should spend a couple of days—thinking by this time he would be able to travel. It was his purpose not to remain long among the Wichetaws, but to return to the timbered country, where we could hunt.

"After the expiration of the time allowed above for rest, he hurried on, that he might soon return, to the hunting grounds —his health continued to improve. On the second morning after the meeting noticed above, the company left the camp, travelled part of a day—came to a water course, where we encamped two nights and a day, and then set out for the village, at which we arrived, after travelling nearly three days. We came to the village of the Echasi, in the neighborhood of the other villages. Soon after arriving and encamping, the head man of the Echasi, called by the Cherokees, Oo-till-ka, or the man who has a feather in his head, came to the camp, met us as his friends, said that he was very sorry to find the old man so sick, and that he would take him to his lodge, where he could take care of him. He would not talk much to him, for fear of wearying him while sick, but busied himself in providing such nourishing food as he could eat. This chief is very kind to all strangers.

"The next morning after breakfast, the Chief told the company to visit any of the villages, as if at home, without ceremony, and to buy such things as they wished. This they did, visited all the villages and did not return until late in the evening. The following morning after breakfast awhile, a messenger arrived from the Chief of the most remote village, that of the Wichetaws, 4 miles off, inviting the company to his lodge, as he should have something for them to eat. His invitation was accepted and the company, excepting myself and young Guess, who stayed with the old man, accompanied back the messenger, and spent the day with the Wichetaws.

"About noon of this day, Sequoyah became much better and requested that the Chief with whom he was staying, might come into the lodge set apart for him. Oo-till-ka did so, took a seat near by where Sequoyah was seated, and said to him: 'I am glad to see you in my lodge. I am friendly with all of the tribes north of me, and meet them always as friends. I am glad to inform you that, though all these tribes were once at war against each other, they have made treaties of peace and now hold each other so firmly by the hand that nothing can separate them.' He said further, that, on the day previous, he and the principal men of the six neighboring villages, had met together and he was glad to have an opportunity, now, to converse a little with him upon those things about which they had met in council—which were concerning the peace and friendship existing between the different tribes; but as they had no good interpreter, what had already passed was as much as they could expect. Sequoyah seemed to be very weak, he proposed that he should lie down again and rest, which he did.

"Then a messenger came to Oo-till-ka, to inform him of the arrival, at a neighboring village, of a Texan runner, inviting them to meet the Texans in council, near the Waco old-village. —The Chief then told Sequoyah that he would talk more with him in the morning, when he was stronger, but would now go to see the Texan. He left. Sequoyah continued laying until evening, (the chief not having yet returned), when he again set up.

"Sequoyah then inquired of me whether I did not think it would be better for the young men of our company, to return, as they might become sick by remaining in the village? I replied that I should agree in his opinions.

"The next morning Sequoyah said to our company, 'My friends, we are a long way from our homes; I am very sick, and may long remain so before I recover. Tomorrow therefore, I wish you all to return home, but my son and Worm, who will journey on with me. I wish you to consent to my proposal; for should we all continue on and some of you be taken sick, it will not be within our power to give such proper attention.' To this request they acceded, and took leave.

"Sequoyah, his son and myself, then prepared to resume our journey, which we did after Sequoyah had talked a little with the Chief, Oo-till-ka, and made him some presents of tobacco and other small articles.

"At the instance of Sequoyah, we took our former route, on the sixth day arrived at the place selected by him as a camping ground, where we spent four days in hunting and then went on until we came to a water course, at which Sequoyah wished to rest some days for the purpose of bathing himself and that a supply of honey might be obtained. He said, at this place, that his health was improving, but he was afflicted still with pains, and a cough, which had the effect to weaken him. After four days' rest, we made ready to start; He then said to me, 'My friend, we are here, in the wilderness; do not get tired of me, I desire to reach the Mexican country. You know the course.'

Being assured of my willingness to go with him, he requested me to take the course—which I did. Travelling on five days more, he again said to us, 'You will not get tired of me, altho' sick? If I die you can do what seems best, but while alive be guided by me.' Continuing on for ten days, we came to a water course, where we rested four days. A few days after, while encamped on a river, the report of guns was heard and then a drum. In descending the river to discover who were so near us, we came upon a road along which some persons had just passed. When appraised of this, Sequoyah determined to follow on the next morning, and overtake them.

"We then took the road and when we overtook them, found them to be Shawnees, and with whom we encamped that night. The next morning the Shawnees inquired of Sequoyah, where he was going? He replied, that he had a great anxiety to visit the country of the Mexicans, but should return in a short time. The Shawnees stated that they were on a hunting expedition, that he could proceed on his way and, if he found any thing interesting, they would be glad to hear it on his return. He then inquired of them the direction of the nearest Mexican towns, or villages? which they pointed out in the same course, Sequoyah remarked, that I had been pointing. We then started and traveled six days in succession, when we stopped—with the intention of hunting a few days, but the old man determined to proceed directly on until we came to a large water course. We proceeded on until a while after sun up, and having crossed a mountain, we came to a small branch but passed on, till we reached a very beautiful, bubbling spring, where the company halted. While still mounted, a number of bees came to the spring, when Sequoyah said, 'As we are neither runaways nor in such a hurry, but that we can stop and look for some honey;' and requested me to hand him some water.

"We encamped at the spring—soon after pulling the saddles off our horses, Young Guess walked away a short distance, and found a bee tree. We spent two nights at this spring. The second night that we encamped there, some Tewockenee Indians came upon us, and stole all our horses; we pursued some distance and could probably have overtaken them, but were afraid to leave the old man long alone, and so returned to the camp. The next morning he requested us to take him to some safe hiding place; to secrete our effects in the tops of trees, and proceed straight to the village of the Tewockenees. After complying with the first part of his request, he altered his determination, and told us not to go in search of our horses which might be some time or other recovered, but to proceed directly to the Mexican settlements, where probably we could obtain other horses.

"We set out on foot in the evening, leaving the old man alone. Travelling on some four miles, Young Guess and myself came to a river called Mauluke, which could not be crossed. We ascended it some distance, until late in the evening and then encamped for the night: in the morning made a raft, crossed the river, proceeded that day a short distance, and again encamped. About noon, the day following, while eating, the reports of many guns were heard in the direction of our route. We immediately proceeded on at a rapid rate till we cleared the mountains and, coming to a prairie, saw the tracks of a wagon.—Here we halted and spent some time, I having advised my companion that we had perhaps, better not proceed to the town until towards night.

"I felt convinced that we were lost, but was unwilling to express an indisposition to proceed on, lest my companion should consider me cowardly. We however, pushed on until we came within about one hundred yards of the town, when hearing a good deal of talking, we stopped and, listening, heard none but the Spanish language. Having turned around and walked back a short distance, we encamped for the night, determined not to go into the Fort until morning. This night we did not sleep much as the firing of guns was kept up throughout the night. The place was San Antonio. In the morning, proceeding into Town, we were not perceived by any one until we got in some distance, when we met with two soldiers, who came up, shook our hands friendly and requested us to follow them. We did so, until met by an officer who, inviting the soldiers and ourselves to follow him, conducted us around a considerable portion of San Antonio to a store, where the people were drinking. The officer having entered the store for a few seconds, told us to follow him to the quarters of the commanding officer, and informed us that we were then in a situation that we could do nothing, intimating that we were prisoners.

"Upon entering the quarters of the commanding officer, he seated himself upon the opposite side of the room from that occupied by ourselves and the soldiers and others who crowded around us. Remaining silent for sometime, and then pacing the room to and fro, this officer at length, came to us and inquired, of what tribe we were, and when informed, declared that he did not at all like the Cherokees, because they had been, a short time previous warring against the Texans. When apprised, that we resided on the Arkansas, within the limits of the U.S., and that we wished to borrow horses, ours having been stolen by the Tewockenees, he repeated his dislike of the Cherokees, and said, he had no horses to lend, and that the Tewockenees and other tribes, some of whom were doubtless prowling about the neighborhood that day, had stolen many of their horses. He further inquired, whether we had any pass-ports? and when told none, said, they were necessary. To which it was replied, that we were ignorant of the fact, as we had frequently visited the towns and settlements of the whites in Arkansas, without ever having any demanded of us. We were also told by him that they would have fired upon and killed us had it not been for the *caps* on our heads, which alone saved us, as the neighboring tribes go with bare heads.

"Sometime was spent in conversation with the officer, who became quite friendly, and gave us tobacco, pass-ports, and a very good axe, that we might bring thereafter a quantity of honey. He also admonished us to be on our guard, in going about the country, as there were many hostile persons among the wild tribes. We then parted.

"In going through the town some of the women called and invited us to take something to eat, but we told them we could not, being in a great hurry—soon after leaving the town, met three or four soldiers, riding very sorry ponies, who also told us to be on the lookout, as there were many Comanches about. After leaving them we began to travel pretty fast, and kept increasing our speed until we got into a run, and throwing away the borrowed axe—travelled a great distance that day,

*"Se-Quo-Yah Teaching Ah-Yo-Keh the Alphabet," by Miss C. S. Robbins.
From George E. Foster,* Se-Quo-Yah, the American Cadmus and Modern
Moses (*Philadelphia, 1885*)

Sequoyah's cabin in Indian Territory

for fear that the Texans might intend to entrap or take some advantage of us.

"The day after leaving San Antonio, we arrived at the camp of Sequoyah, who was well and fast gaining strength. He then requested we should procure him a good supply of provisions, find a secure retreat and set out again, for the Mexican settlements to get horses. A safe retreat was found some three miles from the encampment; he was placed in it and a supply of honey and venison sufficient to last him twenty days procured. The secure retreat was in a cave, which seemed to be above high water; but in case that it should not be, there was a log which he could climb up easily to a more elevated place. Having placed him in this cave, we set out, and travelled on two days; on the third day, which was windy, just as we were approaching a cedar thicket, I happened to look behind, and saw three men coming upon us at full speed. We fell back upon a small patch of timber and threw down our packs for the purpose of defending ourselves; as they came near, I hailed them, and enquired in the Comanche language, if they were friends? They said they were, and immediately threw down their lances and arrows, and came up and shook hands with us, and said as we are friends we will sit down and smoke the pipe.

"The Comanches then said, that when they first saw us they supposed us to be Texans by having on caps, but when they got nearer and saw feathers in them, they took us to be Shawnees or Delawares, and that had it not been for the feathers in our caps, they would have fired upon us. This was the second time that feathers in our caps had probably saved our lives—and they had just been placed there by young Guess, who had killed a turkey. After smoking, one of the Comanches returned for their women whom they had left, upon discovering our tracks. They then inquired where we were going, and when informed, said that our route would be very rough and mountainous; but as they were going there themselves, if well, we would all travel together, as they would be able to show us a nearer and better route. This we consented to and travelled with them three days; we then separated, and travelled fourteen consecutive days before reaching the frontier settlements of Mexico. Before reaching the town we came to a river that we could not cross and had to encamp. Not being aware whether we were near any habitations or not, it caused us so much anxiety that we could not sleep—when some time in the night we heard a drum.

"In the morning we rose early, and there happening to be a turkey seated on a tree near by, young Guess shot it. This we hastily prepared and ate. Soon as this was over we attempted to cross the river, but could not; we then set about making a raft, but just as we had a couple of logs, a mounted Mexican appeared on the opposite bank—inquired who we were, and informed us that there was a ferry lower down. On arriving at the ferry we found the boat ready and a company of armed men in attendance. After crossing, an officer informed us that he would go with us to the principal man of the town, which was about six miles distant; on reaching the town we observed many women washing, who as well as men and boys, immediately gathered around us, being entire strangers, and conducted us into the town. The officer stated the crowd was attracted by curiosity to see us as we were strangers; but had no intention to harm us. He conducted us to the head man of the place. We were led into the house of this man—the crowd that followed us and one that came meeting us, having stopped, at what we supposed to be the limits allowed them.

"The town was small—the houses made of large brick—the people dressed in different kinds of costumes. The houses looked odd, being low with flat roofs. Many of the women were very pretty. Thirteen officers were present. Much time was spent in looking up an Interpreter, who was a Spaniard, that spoke English. Soon as the Interpreter came, the Officer enquired who we were? And being informed, said he was glad to see us, and asked our notions and what object we had in view in visiting Mexico, and also if there were any news of importance from the Texans, whom, *he said* the Mexicans had a short time before defeated in battle, and taken some three hundred of them prisoners. Having satisfied him on these points, and given him to understand that we had not been despatched to his town on any special business of a public nature, he expressed the pleasure it gave him and the other officers to see us, and insisted on our remaining that night in the town, as the day was too far gone for us to reach the Cherokee village, which he informed us, was some thirty miles distant. He then had us conducted to a lodging place in the quarters of some soldiers, telling us to call before leaving in the morning, to receive passports.

"We remained some time in the house assigned us, and then took seats outside it, to observe the people and the soldiery, and sentinels on duty. While thus passing away the time, a Mexican approached me silently and touched my back in order to attract my attention towards him. I looked around, and beheld, pierced through with a stick that he had in his hands, a couple of human ears, taken from one of four persons they had killed a short time before. An officer then came and requested us to walk about the town with him; we complied and followed him about for some time.—He conducted us, amongst other places, into a bake shop and into two or three houses, in each of which he gave us to drink of ardent spirits, which he called whisky, but which tasted very different from any we had ever before drunk. Before we had wandered much about the town, I felt lost, owing to the striking resemblance between its different parts. It being after the hour of twelve o'clock, there was but little business doing, as nearly all of the shops were closed. While yet rambling about the place, a soldier came, to request us to go back to our lodgings, upon reaching which we found the soldiers on parade, ready to march off a short distance. By invitation we joined them and kept along with them, until we came to a kind of public square, where there were a number of large kettles containing bread, beef and soup.

"From these large pots the waiters served the officers, ourselves, and the soldiers in order, by taking up pieces of meat with a fork and giving it to us in our hands. What was given me I ate through politeness, but with some difficulty, so highly seasoned was it with pepper, some of which I was so unfortunate as to get into my eyes. Early the next morning we met with a man who spoke English, and who conducted us to a place where we obtained a breakfast that an Indian could eat without cost, for the man who gave it to us said that he could not be behind the Cherokees; he had been much among them without any expense, he could not therefore charge us; but hoped that we would take our meals with him while we remained there.

"This day, we remained in town, but having passports, left the following morning, in company with a Mexican, who went with us to a town called by the Mexicans, 'San Cranto,' some thirty miles distant. Upon arriving at San Cranto, we were informed that there were a couple of Cherokees in the place, but thinking it would be difficult to find them, we went with our Mexican companion to the house of his brother where we spent the night and by good luck met with our countryman. It gave us great pleasure to see this man, whose name is Standing Rock. He answered a great many questions, and assured us that it would give the Cherokees in Mexico great joy to see their brothers among them, and proposed to accompany us forthwith to their village, about ten miles distant. About seven miles from San Cranto we passed through a small settlement of runaway negroes, some two or three of whom I met with spoke the Cherokee language. Three miles further we arrived at the Cherokee village, situated within a large prairie, in a grove of timber, half a mile wide, and some three miles long, and watered by means of a ditch, from a large spring, some two miles distant.

"Our brothers were very glad to see us, and gave us a warm welcome to their little village. Being soon apprised that we came to obtain assistance, to convey in the aged Sequoyah, who was very anxious to visit them, they declared their readiness to afford us company, but could not furnish any horses, as all of their's, save those that were very poor, had died, since they went into Mexico. They, however, promised to borrow some of the horses belonging to the Mexican army, at a neighboring town. But there being none, the commanding officer referred us back to San Cranto, to which place we returned, after two days' rest-ing with the Cherokees. The officer there could lend us but one horse, the others having been taken off a few days before, to some other post, but supplied us, without solicitation, with bread, meat, salt, sugar and coffee, for the journey. The company then, consisting of nine persons, immediately set off with the borrowed horse—crossed the river again at the ferry, and after constant travelling, on the seventeenth night, camped within a few miles of Sequoyah's cave. Much solicitude was felt by us, for the safety of the old man, as we saw much 'sign' of the wild Indians on our way. Three men were accordingly sent on in advance, to the Cave, with provisions to relieve his wants, if still alive, and in need.

"Mau-luke, we crossed on a raft. Shortly after passing over a very rocky country, we came upon a trail made by wild cattle and horses through a cedar thicket, and along which we discovered the tracks of a man, going in a different direction from ours. These tracks we soon discovered to be those of Sequoyah, from the fact of his being lame. This caused myself and another of the company to hasten to the cave, and gave us no little anxiety, as we discovered that several persons had been but recently along our way.

"Arriving at the cave, we met with our advance company, and discovered a log of wood leaning against a tree, and a letter bound to one of its limbs. The Letter was written by Sequoyah in his own native language, and informed us that, after being left alone, he had met with misfortune—the water having rose very high, drove him from his retreat and swept away his store of provisions and almost everything else; that, under these circumstances he had determined to pursue his journey; that if not too long absent we would be able to find him, as he would fire the grass along his way and the smoke would arise, and that he hoped, although out of provisions, to be able to support life until overtaken by us, as he had cut off meat from the heads of some deer skins. He had no gun, although persuaded to take one when setting out, but relied upon our rifles. We had now great hopes of soon overtaking him, as he had been gone but four days. After reading the letter, we immediately started in pursuit, tracked him to the Mauluke, which he had crossed on a raft.

"We left this camp and returned to our companions—tracked him to the river, saw where he had sat down, followed down the river and came to a raft he had crossed on; we crossed at the same place, came to one of his former camping grounds, and saw where a horse had been tied; feeling confident that he must have obtained a horse by some means or other, we followed on very fast to another camping ground, where we saw bones, which assured us that he had obtained food likewise. There were many speculations, how he had come by the horse and provisions, some surmising one thing and some another.— From the constant rapidity with which we pushed on, and our long journey, the Mexican horse as well as myself began to get tired; I then selected two men, and sent them ahead, while the rest encamped for the night. The two men kept on until night coming on, they lost his track near a creek, but did not stop, hoping to discover a light. They however passed by his camp, as they supposed from the appearance of the sign late in the evening, and returned. In passing near the river, they heard a horse neigh, and then penetrating into the centre of a thicket in the forks of the river, found him seated by a lonely fire. He was greatly rejoiced to meet them. One of the men remained with him while the other returned, and conducted us next evening to his camp. He expressed the great happiness our return gave him; and said that his mind was relieved of much anxiety, as he had suffered much from sickness, and his lonely situation —fearing that his son and myself had either met with some accident or been killed.

"Again expressing the happiness our return gave him, he observed, that for two days past, he had as much provision as desired, and that we must have remarked his mode of travelling, which was brought about under the following circumstances. While engaged, he said, in making a raft to cross the Mauluke, that he might continue on towards Mexico, he suddenly took a notion that he would walk to the summit of a neighboring hill. Throwing down his tomahawk, he started up the hill, and just as the top was gained, to his great surprise, he came close upon three men, who quickly halting, one of them declared themselves to be 'Delawares,' and to which he replied, 'I am a Cherokee.' They camped with him that night, and gave him some of their victuals and partook of his honey. In the morning, the Delawares said to him, 'Come, let us now return to our own villages, we will take you to your door,' He replied, 'No, I have sent forward two young men to the Mexican country, whom I shortly expect back; I am anxious to visit that country. Go with me there. We will shortly return to our own country.' Finding that they could not agree, the Delawares said, that they would remain with him until they killed for him some meat, which they did. While they were hunting, he wrote a letter for them to convey home. Being aged and crippled, the Delawares, when about to part with him, generously gave him a horse to ride.

" 'Such,' said Sequoyah, 'was the way he came by the horse' —and that he would now tell us what happened to him at the cave.

"The twelfth night after we left, the rain poured down and the water came into his cave. He placed all his effects upon a rock in the cave which the water soon surrounded and forced him on a large log. This in turn being moved by the water, he climbed the log, which his son and myself had leaned against the side of the cave and sought refuge in the ledge of the rock— having abandoned everything but a couple of blankets he tied around him; his flint, steel, and spunk and a few small articles that he could get into his pockets. From the ledge of rocks he succeeded in making his way out of the cave and ascending to the top of the hill, where he spent the night under a tree and in unceasing rain. In the morning, finding a dry place, he kindled a fire, by which he warmed himself and dried his clothing, and then went to look at his former home, but found it still covered with water.

"Two days after, he again returned and found that everything had been swept away. But following down the branch he found his saddle bags, around a little tree, from which he recovered all his papers and other things, and also a tent and three blankets; and on the day following a brass kettle. After this he made no further search—giving up all for lost; but even felt glad to escape as well as he did, especially with his life which he said was far more precious than aught else. The water having swept away his supply of food, he was now left entirely without, and when he could get nothing else, lived on what little flesh he could shave off from the skins of deer killed by us before leaving. During the greater part of the time however, he ate nothing but wild honey, which he obtained from a couple of large trees, that he fortunately discovered and felled at the expense of repeated efforts, with a small tomahawk. His health had not been good, but such he said, as would have confined almost any one to his bed. For each day that we were absent, before leaving his cave, he cut a notch in a large oak tree.

"We remained four or five days at the camp, where we found Sequoyah and in the vicinity, until a stock of provision was killed, and then resumed our journey, and after travelling sixteen days forded the river mentioned before, near the Mexican village. In a few days more, halting along for a short time at the different towns, where Sequoyah received the kindest hospitality from the Mexicans, the company arrived at the Cherokee village.

"The Worm spent some time with the Cherokees and then returned at the solicitation of Sequoyah, with a party of Caddoes, to the Wichitaw town to recover, if possible, the horses that had been stolen from them. He was unable to get them, and not meeting with any person going to Mexico, could not return early as expected. At length several Caddoes arrived from Mexico and brought tidings that Sequoyah was no more, which was soon confirmed by a party of Cherokees. The complaint that terminated his life, was the cough which had long afflicted him, combined perhaps with some disease common in that country. His death was sudden—having been long confined to the house, he requested one day some food, and while it was preparing breathed his last."

The next year after Sequoyah's departure from home, the Cherokee National Council, on October 25, 1843, passed an act authorizing the publication of a national newspaper to be called the *Cherokee Advocate*. It had for its object the diffusion of important news among the Cherokee people, the advancement of their general interest, and defense of Indian rights. It was to be published both in English and in the Cherokee language in the characters of Sequoyah's invention. The editor was to be selected by the national council, and he was to publish all laws and treaties affecting the Indians.

Five days after the enactment of the measure establishing the *Cherokee Advocate* an act was passed declaring all the salt springs in the Cherokee Nation to be the property of the Nation to which a rental or royalty thereafter would have to be paid for their use. However, with a continued sense of obligation to the long absent Sequoyah, it was expressly provided that his salt spring was excepted from the operation of this law, so that he could continue to make salt there rent free.

The first issue of the *Cherokee Advocate* appeared September 26, 1844. The paper contained four pages of six columns each. It was a useful organ of the Cherokee people, who found in it all the laws currently enacted by their national council and much other valuable information, besides the news of the day. Publication of the *Advocate* was suspended for lack of funds September 28, 1853, and was not resumed until April 26, 1870. With slight interruptions it was published from that time until 1906.

Preceding the *Advocate* by a few weeks was the *Cherokee Messenger,* printed on the Baptist Mission press a few miles north of where is now Westville, Oklahoma. Twelve numbers in English and the Cherokee characters of Sequoyah appeared from August, 1844, to May, 1846. The first number contained much information about Sequoyah's alphabet and instructions concerning the principles involved, to facilitate the study of it.

About two weeks after the first issue of the *Cherokee Advocate* members of the Cherokee National Council met in regular session in October, 1844. Proud of their national newspaper, their thoughts naturally turned to Sequoyah, more than any other man responsible for their progress on the road to literacy. He had been gone more than two years.

"But what," their anxiety was expressed in the columns of the *Advocate,* "has become of this remarkable man, whose native genius has struck light from darkness—conferred inconceivable blessings upon his people and achieved for his own name an enviable distinction among those few truly great names, with which are connected imperishible honor? is he still alive? or does his venerable head repose beneath some unknown clod of the Grand Prairie? These are questions that we cannot now, satisfactorily answer.

"The Council of this Nation," continued the *Advocate,* "out of respect for his character and in consideration of his great invention, have allowed him, for many years, an annual pension." When this pension was inaugurated is not stated, but December 29, more than a year after Sequoyah departed from the Cherokee Nation the national council passed an act providing that "in lieu of the sum allowed to George Guess, in consideration of his invention of the Cherokee alphabet, passed December 10th, 1841, and which is hereby repealed, the sum of three hundred dollars to be paid to the said George Guess out of the National Treasury, annually, during his natural life." It provided also that in the event of the death of Guess the pension should be paid to his wife Sally Guess annually as long as she should live. Annual appropriations were accordingly made thereafter to meet the payments of the pension, and in 1853 when financial difficulties had greatly depreciated the value of Cherokee warrants, the council, with a strict sense of obligation, passed an act directing the treasurer of the nation to pay Sally Guess cash for the warrant issued to her December 16, 1852. This was probably the first literary pension in American history, and certainly the first and only one ever granted by an Indian tribe.

Continued the *Advocate's* account of Sequoyah's wanderings: "Several reports concerning him, have reached his friends in this country. That which seems to be most probable, when the hardships to which in his wanderings, he has been necessarily exposed are remembered in addition to his decrepit form, and the weight of many years, is that this truly great man full of years and of honors, sleeps the sleep *of Death,* in some wild and unknown spot, far from his wife, his country, and his people."

Anxious to discover the whereabouts of their long absent countryman, the Cherokees applied to Indian Agent Pierce M. Butler for funds with which to finance a search for him. Butler, on November 23, presented the matter to the secretary of war, who, on January 17, 1845, authorized the expenditure of $200 of tribal funds in the effort to discover Sequoyah and bring him home.

The Cherokees were delighted, said the *Advocate,* with the provisions "for tracing up the venerable wanderer and restoring him to his family and country. Governor Butler feels the liveliest interest in the destiny of George Guess, whose name shall be forever enshrined in the affections of his whole people. He will take immediate measures to carry out the designs of the War Department, which receive our sincere acknowledgements and which we ardently hope may be crowned with entire success. There is no event, we are persuaded, that would afford more heartfelt joy to the Cherokees at large, than to have their distinguished countryman among them once more."

Apparently the messengers who were to look for Sequoyah had not departed on their errand March 6, 1845, for on that day the *Advocate* carried the following information: "George Guess. —Recent intelligence has been received which renders it highly probable that the inventor of the Cherokee alphabet has not, as is generally supposed, been gathered to his fathers, but is still among the living. If the intelligence be correct, he is now with some of his countrymen, who are living near Matamoros, Mexico. Some Cherokees are supposed to leave this country, in the course of a short time for Matamoros, for the purpose of restoring him to his country, if still alive."

Further information touching the fate of Sequoyah and the search for him is disclosed by the following statement of some of his companions on their route home, to Cherokee Agent Pierce M. Butler: "Warren's Trading House, Red River, April 21st, 1845. We, the undersigned Cherokees, direct from the

Spanish dominions, do hereby certify, that George Guess, of the Cherokee Nation, Arkansas, departed this life in the town of Sanfernando in the month of August, 1843, and his son (Chusaleta) is at this time on the Brasas River, Texas, about 30 miles above the falls, and intends returning home this fall.

"Given under our hands day and date above written. Standing Rock [by mark], Standing Bowles [by mark], Watch Justice [by mark], Witness: Daniel G. Watson, Jesse Chisholm."

There is also the later report in the characters of Sequoyah's invention to Agent Butler by Oo-no-leh, one of the messengers sent to search for him. The report, as translated into English reads as follows: "P. M. Butler Cherokee Agent, Sir; After reaching Red River on my way, I met with the following Cherokees from Mexico:—Jesse, the leader of the party, The Worm, Gah-na-nes-kee, The Standing Man and The Standing Rock. The last named, The Standing Rock, attended Sequoyah during his last sickness and also witnessed his death and burial. Isse-sa-de-tah, the son of Sequoyah, remains on Red River. He is very sorry that the remains of his father are buried so far from his own country, and remains where he is on this account.

"As Sequoyah was the object for which I had started in search, and having learned the fact of his death which I am communicating to those who sent me, it will be useless for me to proceed further. I will return toward home. He is dead without a doubt. His remaining family, widow, two daughters and a young man live somewhere in Skin Bayou District.

"Bayou District, 15th May, 1845.   Oo-no-leh."

The personality, occupation and environment of this remarkable Indian are elusive, particularly before 1821 when he completed his invention. He was obviously possessed of a strong sense of public concern and duty which with an active and brilliant mind brought forth his great work. No writer about Sequoyah has ever before mentioned his military service, which introduces a new phase of character. This occupation, his wedding to Sally, participation in the treaty council of 1816, his journey to Arkansas in 1818, are meager hints of some of the other things that engaged the attention and energies of Guess during the nine years he was working on his alphabet.

And what about his lameness? Observers and writers have said that he was lame from disease since childhood. But it is hard to believe a cripple would have been accepted in the army; this suggests the thought that he was wounded in the service, but the records in the war department contradict that supposition. The picture of this Indian philosopher limping along with his company into battle from a strong sense of public duty is an intriguing one at least.

The late W. J. Weaver of Fort Smith said he knew Sequoyah and his family well. When they lived about fifteen miles from Fort Smith on Skin Bayou in Sequoyah district, Cherokee Nation, from 1839 to 1842 he often enjoyed the hospitality of their cabin home in his rides in the vicinity, and traded with them in his store in Fort Smith for their products, "such as honey, butter, eggs, chickens, deer and coon skins which they exchanged for family supplies; but they never bought any whiskey, and I think they were strictly temperate."

Mr. Weaver wrote of Sequoyah at some length for his paper, the Fort Smith *Elevator,* retailing much that was already in print or set forth here. Unfortunately he did not tell much of his impressions of the Indian. He did say, however, that he would have been taken for a full-blood. Differing with other observers, he said "he was quiet and morose in manner and would not talk English, but he understood it; in this respect he was like many other Indians, who would speak to you in their language and understand you in English. His wife was different. She was affable, pleasant, talkative, and spoke the English language fluently, and it was from her that I learned much of George's history." She lived in the neighborhood many years after the death of her husband. "She was a good housekeeper; she was always dressed in homespun wear, and had a loom. In fact at that time many of the Cherokees were expert in spinning, weaving and coloring, and seldom bought any clothing but 'ontnowo yunago' (white domestic) for underwear. George always wore the conventional homespun hunting shirt trimmed with red fringe, with a red shawl twisted around his head as a turban. Tessee, his son, was grown to manhood, and his daughter was about seventeen, both unmarried, when their father went to Mexico. The family lived comfortably on their farm and had ponies, cattle and hogs on the range." After his return from Mexico Tessee related to Mr. Weaver interesting accounts of their wanderings, which unfortunately were not preserved.

Heroic and pathetic was the figure of this man groping in the dark for something he had never seen; an objective only vaguely conceived, but something he very definitely believed he could bring into being for the great good of his people. Toiling, striving patiently alone, with no human being to bear him company, none to understand or encourage, none with whom he could communicate or ask counsel; unable to read in any lan-

73

guage and therefore unable to call to his aid any of the accumulated wisdom and experience of the white man. By his industry and perseverance incurring the misunderstanding, ridicule and hostility of those he was trying to serve.

Ignorant of the writings and teachings of white philosophers, Sequoyah hit upon the great truth, and what to him was an original discovery, that enlightenment and civilization of a people would progress and develop in proportion as they were able to express themselves and preserve their ideas upon the written and printed page, and exchange these ideas, one with another by this medium.

For the instruction and enlightenment of the people many temperance and other tracts, primers, spelling books, arithmetics, annual almanacs, passages from the Scriptures, catechisms, hymn books, and other publications were printed in whole or in part with the type of Sequoyah on the Mission press at Park Hill. The same characters were used in the printing of the constitution and laws of the Cherokee Nation in various editions, resolutions of the national council, messages of the chiefs, on the national press at Tahlequah, the capital, from which issued the *Cherokee Advocate*. Even the current acts of the legislative council were printed in this same medium and promptly circulated among all the people who read them with interest and profit.

As a result, the Cherokees became better informed of their laws and the actions of their public servants than members of any other Indian tribe. Published in fairly limited editions, in the main nearly one hundred years ago, few of these prints are to be seen outside occasional libraries of collectors and great public institutions, where they are reserved among the rare books. A quantity of the Cherokee type used on the national Press is now deposited in the United States National Museum at Washington.

Thinking of Sequoyah and his achievements the mind is bewildered in trying to conceive the background that produced this miracle. While it is agreed that his mother was an Indian woman of the Cherokee tribe, conflicting theories of the paternity of Sequoyah have flowed from the pens of many writers. After weighing all the evidence the account given here is believed to be authentic and plausible.

The most convincing testimony on the point made contemporaneously with the living Sequoyah was the previously quoted statement by Gen. Ethan Allen Hitchcock while he was in the Cherokee Nation in 1841, where he met and observed Sequoyah. Like many others he was curious about the parentage of this remarkable man. He wrote in his diary what he heard on the point from the lips of Chief John Ross.

Some writers have subscribed to the wholly improbable and unauthenticated theory that Sequoyah's father was a vagabond itinerant German named George Gist, whose rovings brought him in the Cherokee Nation. That the amazing genius of this remarkable Indian must have been sired by a man of vastly superior qualifications is obvious.

Such a man was Nathaniel Gist, a friend of George Washington, who spent many years among the Cherokees in the capacity of hunter, explorer, and soldier. Their attachment to Gist had induced them to give him Long Island, a valuable holding in the Little Tennessee River. So intimate was he with the Indians that his loyalty to the whites came under suspicion and it required an official inquiry by the governor and general assembly of Virginia to clear him of the charge of aiding the Cherokees in their hostilities against the whites. The council made its findings December 17, 1776, vindicating Gist and in less than a month he was commissioned colonel of a regiment in the Continental Army. Washington then sent him to the Cherokees to secure recruits for the army and he brought seventeen warriors to Virginia to fight for the Colonies against Great Britain.

The arguments that have been adduced relating to this subject are much too extended to be set out here but they are sufficient in the mind of the Author to establish that the father of Sequoyah could not have been the German clod whose existence even is not established, but must have been Nathaniel Gist, progenitor of many other distinguished Americans.

Nathaniel Gist was married in 1783 to Judith Cary Bell and by this union were born several daughters who married prominent men: One, Sarah Howard Gist, married Jesse Bledsoe, United States senator from Kentucky; Anne Cary Gist married Dr. Joseph Boswell; Eliza Gist married Francis Preston Blair, distinguished journalist, publicist and editor of the Washington *Globe;* they were the parents of Montgomery Blair, a member of Lincoln's cabinet, and Francis Preston Blair, Jr., United States senator from Missouri and a brigadier-general in the Civil War; Maria C. Gist, a fourth daughter of Nathaniel Gist, married Benjamin Gratz, a wealthy citizen of Lexington.

Francis P. Blair, Jr., was the Democratic candidate for vice president with Seymour in 1868; and B. Gratz Brown was the

Democratic candidate for the same office on the ticket with Horace Greeley in 1872. Major Gist Blair, son of Lincoln's postmaster general, owns and occupies the historic and interesting old Blair home on Pennsylvania Avenue in Washington. He cherishes many authentic family traditions of kinship to Sequoyah, with which he has generously aided the Author.

In the Bureau of American Ethnology in Washington is a letter written by John Mason Brown of the Louisville bar, a descendant of Nathaniel Gist, who stated that Sequoyah had visited the Gist descendants in Kentucky, probably on his way to or from Washington in 1828; on this occasion he was looking up his white kin. Maj. Gist Blair told the Author that when he was a youth about 1878, he went to Kentucky to see some of the Gratz relatives and there learned of the accepted fact that Sequoyah was the son of Nathaniel Gist.

Major Blair hopes to discover the names and records of the seventeen Cherokees who enlisted with Nathaniel Gist and aid in enrolling their male descendants in the Sons of the American Revolution, of which he is an active and prominent member.

The witnesses quoted in this sketch not only strongly support the Nathaniel Gist theory of the paternity of Sequoyah, but make his birthday nearer the birth of our country than 1760 or thereabouts, a date frequently ascribed to Sequoyah. The latter date would make him 53 years old when in 1813, he enlisted for service in the Creek War. It is much easier to believe he was then under 40, as he would have been if he had been born in 1773 or later, than to believe that on the waning side of middle age he went to war.

The name and fame of Sequoyah have been recorded in

honorable remembrance and still survive, long after his alphabet has passed into the realm of historic *curioso,* while its influence continues as a vital force in the civilization of Oklahoma. In 1851 the Cherokee Council changed the name of Skin Bayou District in which Sequoyah lived to Sequoyah District. Substantially the same area became Sequoyah County of the new state of Oklahoma. For this great Indian was named the giant redwood tree of California, and in 1902 the Sequoya League, with headquarters in California, designed to improve the conditions of all Indians.

During the summer of 1905 a convention of representative citizens of the Indian Territory, Indians and whites, at Muskogee wrote a constitution for a proposed state of the Union which they named Sequoyah. This document, signalizing the first political co-operation of the Indians and whites was submitted for popular vote of the people of the Indian Territory and adopted by a majority of more than 47,000. However, it was rejected by the national administration in favor of a plan for a state to be composed of the union of Indian Territory and Oklahoma Territory two years later.

In 1911 when Oklahoma was four years old, the legislature provided for the placing of a statue of Sequoyah in Statuary Hall in the National Capitol. A contract for the making of the statue was entered into with the sculptor Vinnie Ream. Protracted ill health prevented her from executing the commission, and after her death in 1916 her husband, General Hoxie, requested the Washington sculptor George Julian Zolnay to take over the contract. Given a free hand in planning the work, he undertook it enthusiastically. The garb worn by the Sequoyah of Statuary Hall is not that of the Sequoyah of history, but the reason is explained by Mr. Zolnay in a letter to the Author: "It might also interest you to know that one of the determining factors of success, both artistically and historically, was my determination to use the blanket which is highly characteristic and invests the statue with a dignity no other treatment could have given it." In making the statue Mr. Zolnay used as a model Miss Ann Ross, a Cherokee of Oklahoma, great granddaughter of Chief John Ross, who helped him, he said, in catching the racial characteristics of the subject. This classic statue was unveiled and presented by Oklahoma to the United States on June 6, 1917, with appropriate addresses and other proceedings in Statuary Hall, in the Senate and in the House.

When Sequoyah departed for Mexico in 1843 the home in which he left his family was a log cabin. A set of house logs cut by him, with which he planned to build another room, lay near by. In 1855, the year she presented her bounty claim to the Indian Office, Guess's widow sold the property to another Cherokee named George Blair, who constructed the additional room so that his home became a double log house with a huge stack chimney between the two rooms. Mr. Blair died in 1887 at the age of ninety-eight years and his remains lie in the little family cemetery near by. Among his survivors was a son Thomas, who was born in 1844 and died in 1932.

In 1930 the Author of this sketch visited the Sequoyah-Blair home and secured pictures and a statement concerning its history from Mr. Thomas Blair. He was eleven years old when his father bought it and not only recalled the transaction, Mrs. Guess, and her children, but remembered the things his father told him touching the history of the place. He recalled that after the sale Mrs. Guess and her two children removed to another home a few miles southwest and the Blair family occupied the Sequoyah improvements. These things the Author reduced to writing which was signed by Mr. Blair and filed in the archives of the Oklahoma Historical Society. This statement, with the result of other investigations and study, was employed by him in the press of Oklahoma and other quarters in promoting a movement for the preservation of the Sequoyah home.

In 1936 Judge R. L. Williams, Hon. W. W. Hastings and the Author took steps to this end. Title to ten acres of land, including the Sequoyah home, was secured in the name of the State of Oklahoma for the use and benefit of the Oklahoma Historical Society. Approval of a Federal Works Progress Administration project was secured, under which was performed all the work of construction now in evidence at the Sequoyah shrine. The north room, constructed by Mr. Blair after Sequoyah left the country, was torn down and the original log cabin enclosed in a handsome stone structure. The logs of the north room were employed in the construction of a custodian's lodge near the entrance. Water works, a toilet and lighting system have been installed and the whole ten acres enclosed by a handsome stone wall. For the purchase of the material that went into this shrine, donations amounting to more than $4,000 were made by a number of Creek, Seminole, Choctaw, Osage, Quapaw and Cherokee Indians. To the perseverance and industry of Judge Williams much credit is due for the success of this enterprise. The corner stone of the stone building was laid June 13, 1936, with appropriate ceremonies in the presence of thousands of interested citizens, Indians and whites.

At the northern limits of the town of Calhoun, Georgia, stands a monument to Sequoyah, surmounted by a large figure intended to represent the American Cadmus. This was designed and constructed in 1927 by W. L. Hillhouse of Calhoun, and paid for by the Calhoun Woman's Club. Two miles east of this monument on the Chatsworth road is the site of New Echota, the former capitol of the Cherokee Nation, where stood the printing office of the *Cherokee Phoenix*. On this spot is a Cherokee Indian memorial designed and constructed by Mr. Hillhouse, paid for by an act of Congress, and dedicated in 1931. On two faces of the monument are bronze tablets containing information about the Cherokee people; one of these refers to the alphabet invented by Sequoyah and the Cherokee newspaper published there. Through the influence of Robert Sparks Walker of Chattanooga, the old Crutchfield Spring eight miles south of that city, and at the foot of Lookout Mountain, was recently formally re-christened "Sequoyah Spring," by the Cumberlands Hiking Club. He is also heading a movement with promise of success, to change the name of Monroe County, Tennessee, to "Sequoyah County."

Most significant and lasting memorial to the immortal Sequoyah is the learning and culture of a fine body of Americans, the Cherokee people. Their advanced position in society directly traceable to Sequoyah's works, exercised a beneficent influence on other tribes of Indians and contributed substantially to the civilization of the new state of which they are a part.

81

INDEX

A

Absence of Sequoyah: speculation concerning, 69, 70

Act of Union of Cherokee Nation: 35

Alexander, John: describes Sequoyah, 40ff.

Alphabet invented by Sequoyah: 4; number of characters, 39; report on by American Board of Commissioners for Foreign Missions, 7, 12; uses of, 74

American Board of Commissioners for Foreign Missions: appraises Sequoyah alphabet, 7, 12

Arbuckle, Gen. Matthew: 35

Atsi: translates extracts from St. John's Gospel, 11

B

Bee tree: found by Sequoyah's party, 54

Black Fox (Cherokee): 16

Blair, Francis Preston: 76

Blair, George: purchases Sequoyah home, 79

Blair, Maj. Gist: 77

Blair, Montgomery: 76

Blair, Thomas: owner of Sequoyah home, 79

Bledsoe, Jesse: 76

Boswell, Dr. Joseph: 76

Boudinot Elias: 19, 29, edits *Cherokee Phoenix*, 13, 14.

Brainerd Mission: 10

British Museum: file of *Cherokee Phoenix*, 14

Brown, B. Gratz: 76

Brown, David: 11

Brown, John Mason: 77

Bushyhead, Rev. Jesse: 33

Butler, Pierce M., Cherokee agent: 69ff.

Butrick, Daniel S.: 10

C

Cache Creek: 48

Caddo (Indians): 66

Calhoun (Ga.): monument to Sequoyah, 81

Calhoun Woman's Club: 81

Campbell, Archibald: 4, 48

Cherokee Advocate: 19, 28, 74; founded, 67

Cherokee (Indians): benefited by Sequoyah's invention, 74, 81; emigration, 5, 15, 29, 32, 33; on Washita River, 48; with Sequoyah, reach San Antonio, 55; solicitous over Sequoyah's absence; in Mexico, 61; dissension among, 33; of Texas, homes destroyed by Texans, 35; constitution adopted at Tahlequah, 35; treaties, of 1816, 4; 1817, 5; 1828, 16; school system, 31; council votes pension to Sequoyah, 68, 69; council, 15, 34

Cherokee Messenger: 68

Cherokee Phoenix: 14, 19, 24, 31, 81; press seized, 15

Cherokee Phoenix and Indians' Advocate: 15

Chisholm, Jesse (Cherokee): 71

Choctaw Nation: refuge for Cherokees, 35

Comanche (Indians): visited by Sequoyah's party, 57

Coodey, William Shorey: letter about Sequoyah, 17; writes Cherokee Act of Union, 35

D

Death of Sequoyah: 66

Delaware (Indians): 64

Donors to expense of Sequoyah shrine: 80

Drew, John: 4

Dwight Mission: 31, 40, 45

E

Echasi (Oo-till-ka) (Indians): visit Sequoyah, 50, 51, 52

Echota (Cherokee capital): 3

Edwards's Settlement: 48

Evarts, Jeremiah: describes Sequoyah, 28ff.

F

Fort Coffee: 36

Fort Gibson: 36, 40

Fort Loudon: 3

Fort Smith: 36, 40

Fort Wayne: 36

G

Gah-na-nes-kee (Cherokee Indians): 71

Gist, Anne Cary: 76

Gist, Eliza: 76

Gist, Maria C.: 76

Gist, Nathaniel: 76, 77; father of Sequoyah, 75

Gist, Sarah Howard: 76

Going Back (Cherokee Indian): 4

Gratz, Benjamin: 76

Greeley, Horace: 77

Guess, George: 4; *see* Sequoyah

Guess, Sally: 4, 30, 73; to share in Sequoyah pension, 69

Guess, Tessee (son of Sequoyah): 48, 73

H

Hard Mush (Cherokee chief): killed by Texans, 35

Hastings, W. W.: 80

Hicks, Charles R.: 8, 9, 10

Hicks, Elijah: 8, 14

Hillabee: 4

Hillhouse, W. L.: 81

Hitchcock, Asa: 45

Hitchcock, Gen. Ethan Allen: 75; describes Sequoyah, 44, 45

Horseshoe, Battle of: 4

Houston, Samuel: 42

I

Illinois Bayou: 45

Illinois Camp Ground: 33

Isse-sa-de-tah (Tessee): son of Sequoyah, 71

J

Jesse (Cherokee): 71

Jolly, Chief John (Cherokee): 5, 6, 45

K

King, Charles Bird: paints Sequoyah's portrait, 19

Knapp, Samuel Lorenzo: describes Sequoyah and his work, 19ff.

L

Lees Creek: 17, 30

Little River: 48

Lowrey, Maj. George (Cherokee): 3, 8; signs Cherokee Act of Union, 35

M

Mauluke River (Texas): 54; crossed by Cherokees, 62, 64
Maw, John (Cherokee): 35
McKenney, Thomas L.: 9
McLamore, Capt. John (Cherokee): 3
Medal: presented to Sequoyah, 8
Mexico: visited by Cherokees, 61
Military service of Sequoyah: 3, 4, 72
Missionary Herald: 14
Moravian: mission in Cherokee Nation, 9, 10, 11
Morgan, Col. Gideon: 3

N

New Echota (Ga.): 15, 29, 81

O

"Ode to Sequoyah": 82
Oklahoma Historical Society: purchases Sequoyah home, 80
"Old Settlers" ("Western Cherokees"): 33, 34
Oo-no-leh (Cherokee): reports on search for Sequoyah, 71

P

Park Hill: 32, 48
Paternity of Sequoyah: 45ff., 75ff.
Path Killer (Cherokee chief): 8
Payne, John Howard: 8; at home of John Ross, 42ff.; describes Sequoyah, 42ff.
Pension: voted Sequoyah by Cherokee Council, 68
Posey, Alex: "Ode to Sequoyah," 82
Printing press proposed: 13

R

Ream, Vinnie: 78
Red Clay (Tenn.): 15
Red River: 48
Rogers, John (Cherokee chief): 16
Ross, Ann: poses for Sequoyah statue, 79
Ross, Chief John (Cherokee): 4, 8, 14, 15, 29, 33, 34, 35, 75; host to Sequoyah and John Howard Payne, 43ff.

S

Sallisaw Creek: 45
Salt Springs: 17, 30, 67
San Antonio (Tex.): 55
San Cranto: visited by Sequoyah's companions, 61
Schermerhorn, Rev. John F.: 15
Sequoyah: 3, 4, 10; appearance of, 26, 37, 43ff., 73; work described by John Alexander, 40; by John Howard Payne, 42ff.; by General Hitchcock, 44ff.; by Capt. John Stuart, 36; by Samuel Lorenzo Knapp, 19ff.
Sequoyah: emigrates to Arkansas, 5, 6, 18, 24, 45; environment of, 71; military service, 4, 72; paternity of, 45, 75ff.; birth of, 77; activities in West, 16; on delegation to Washington, 16, 18; participates in Cherokee council, 33ff.; promised $500 by treaty, 17; signs Cherokee Act of Union, 35; excites interest in Washington, 19; talent for painting, 27; counsels Cherokees in Texas, 36; home life of, 30, 40; appreciation by Cherokees, 8

84

Sequoyah alphabet: plans by Sequoyah, 5, 10, 11, 19ff.; tested, 25; uses of, 24, 47, 67, 68; excites suspicion of his people, 24, 25; type cast, 13; work on described by his son, 47; work on, 7, 11, 37, 38, 39

Sequoyah departs for Mexico: 48; prostrated by illness, 48, 49; wanderings described, 48ff.; rejoined by companions, 64; driven from cave, 65; kind treatment by Mexicans, 66; companions return to, 57; anxiety over his absence, 68; search for, 69, 70; report of searchers, 70, 71; death of, 66

Sequoyah, memorials of: 78; home purchased by Oklahoma Historical Society, 80; home sold by widow, 79; statues of, 78; proposed state of, 78; district of, 78

Shawnee (Indians): in Texas, 53

Sketch of the Cherokee and Choctaw Indians, A: 36

Skin Bayou (Cherokee Nation): 72

Standing Bowles (Cherokee chief): 71

Stand Watie: 15

Stuart, Capt. John: describes Sequoyah, 36ff.

T

Tahlequah (Cherokee Nation): 33

Takatokah (Double Springs) (Cherokee Nation): 33

Tawakoni (Indians): 54, 56

The Bowle (Cherokee chief): killed by Texans, 35

The Standing Man (Cherokee): 71

The Standing Rock (Cherokee): 61, 71; attended Sequoyah at his death, 71

The Worm (Cherokee): 66, 71; companion of Sequoyah in Texas, 48

Tobacco Will (Cherokee): 16, 44

Trail of Tears: 33

Translations: 10, 11

Treaty Party: 33

Turkeytown: 3

Turtle Fields (Cherokee): 41

Tuskegee: 3

U

Union Mission: 32

V

Vann, Charles H.: 8

Vann, Joseph: 15

W

Waco: Indian village, 51

Walker, Robert Sparks: 81

War of 1812: 3

Watch Justice (Cherokee): 71

Watson, Daniel G.: 71

Weaver, W. J.: describes Sequoyah, 72

Wichita (Indian town): 48, 51, 66

Williams, Judge R. L.: 80

Wills Valley (Cherokee Nation): 12

Worcester, Rev. Samuel A.: 13; reports on Sequoyah alphabet, 12; establishes printing press, 31, 32

Works Progress Administration: constructs Sequoyah shrine, 80

Z

Zolnay, George Julian: 78